THIRTY SETTINGS OF "FORS SEULEMENT"

RECENT RESEARCHES IN THE MUSIC OF THE MIDDLE AGES AND EARLY RENAISSANCE

Margaret Bent, general editor

A-R Editions, Inc., publishes six quarterly series—

Recent Researches in the Music of the Middle Ages and Early Renaissance,
Margaret Bent, general editor;

Recent Researches in the Music of the Renaissance,
James Haar and Howard Mayer Brown, general editors;

Recent Researches in the Music of the Baroque Era,
Robert L. Marshall, general editor;

Recent Researches in the Music of the Classical Era,
Eugene K. Wolf, general editor;

Recent Researches in the Music of the Nineteenth and Early Twentieth Centuries,
Jerald C. Graue, general editor;

Recent Researches in American Music,
H. Wiley Hitchcock, general editor—

which make public music that is being brought to light
in the course of current musicological research.

Each volume in the *Recent Researches* is devoted
to works by a single composer or to a single genre of composition,
chosen because of its potential interest to scholars and performers,
and prepared for publication according to the standards that govern
the making of all reliable historical editions.

Subscribers to this series, as well as patrons of subscribing institutions,
are invited to apply for information about the "Copyright-Sharing Policy"
of A-R Editions, Inc., under which the contents of this volume
may be reproduced free of charge for study or performance.

Correspondence should be addressed:

A-R EDITIONS, INC.
315 West Gorham Street
Madison, Wisconsin 53703

RECENT RESEARCHES IN THE MUSIC OF THE MIDDLE AGES AND
EARLY RENAISSANCE • VOLUME XIV

FORS SEULEMENT

*Thirty Compositions for Three to Five Voices or Instruments
from the Fifteenth and Sixteenth Centuries*

Edited by Martin Picker

A-R EDITIONS, INC. • MADISON

Copyright © 1981, A-R Editions, Inc.

ISSN 0362-3572

ISBN 0-89579-135-6

Library of Congress Cataloging in Publication Data:
Fors seulement
   (Recent researches in the music of the Middle Ages and early Renaissance ; v. 14)
   Originally a 3-part chanson by Johannes Ockeghem ; French words.
   1. Chansons, Polyphonic.   I. Ockeghem, Johannes, d. 1496? Fors seulement (Chanson).   II. Picker, Martin.   III. Series.
M2.R2383   vol. 14   [M1]   81-14887
ISBN 0-89579-135-6   AACR2

Contents

Preface		vii
Texts and Translations		xxviii

Thirty Settings of "Fors seulement"

[1a]	[Johannes] O[c]keghem	*3 voices*	1
[1b]	[Johannes Ockeghem]	*3 voices*	3
[2]	[Johannes] O[c]keghem	*3 voices*	5
[3]	[Jacob] Hobrecht	*4 voices*	8
[4]	[Pierre de la] Rue	*4 voices*	12
[5]	[Matthaeus] Pipelare	*4 voices*	15
[6]	[Antoine Brumel]	*4 voices*	18
[7]	G[illes] Reingot	*4 voices*	22
[8]	[Marbriano] de Orto	*4 voices*	25
[9]	Jo[hannes] Agricola	*4 voices*	28
[10]	[Anonymous]	*4 voices*	31
[11]	Andreas de Sylva	*4 voices*	34
[12]	[Pierre de la] Rue	*5 voices*	37
[13]	[Anonymous]	*5 voices*	42
[14]	[Anonymous]	*5 voices*	47
[15]	[Anonymous]	*5 voices*	50
[16]	[Anonymous]	*5 voices*	53
[17]	Antonius Divitis	*5 voices*	58
[18]	Jacob[us] Roman[us]	*4 voices*	64
[19]	De la Val	*4 voices*	67
[20]	[Johannes] Ghisling [Verbonet]	*4 voices*	70

[21]	[Incertus]	*4 voices*	73
[22]	[Josquin des Prez?]	*4 voices*	76
[23]	[Anonymous]	*5 voices*	80
[24]	[Anonymous]	*3 voices*	84
[25]	[Anonymous]	*4 (5) voices*	86
[26]	[Matthaeus Pipelare]	*4 voices*	89
[27]	[Anonymous]	*4 voices*	92
[28]	Anth[oine] de Févin	*3 voices*	96
[29]	Jörg Blanckenmüller	*3 voices*	98
[30]	Adrianus Willa[e]rt	*5 voices*	101

Preface

Introduction

The fifteenth and sixteenth centuries witnessed the emergence of extensive "families" of musical compositions (including such diverse forms as Masses, motets, chansons, instrumental fantasias, and dances) that derive a significant part of their musical substance from a pre-existent work. Rooted in the medieval tradition of using a plainsong as the basis for a polyphonic composition (a method that was expanded in the thirteenth century to include the borrowing of secular melodies as well), this use of pre-existent melodies was amplified in the fifteenth century to include drawing upon individual voices of pre-existent polyphonic compositions to create new works. Toward the end of the fifteenth century, composers began to adopt a freer approach, embracing all voices of the polyphonic model. In true Renaissance spirit, these musicians often engaged in competition to see who could show the most ingenious manipulation of the same material. Sources for the largest of these "families" of compositions include such popular melodies as the famous "L'homme armé," on which composers from the fifteenth to the seventeenth centuries composed Masses, and Hayne von Ghizeghem's "De tous biens plaine," a secular polyphonic composition that gave rise to over two dozen settings within the single generation from ca. 1475 to 1500.

Probably the largest family of pieces based on a polyphonic model is the one generated by the three-voice *rondeau* "Fors seulement," composed around 1460 by the Flemish chapelmaster of the kings of France, Johannes Ockeghem (d. 1497). Derived from this work, or from one of its descendants, are more than thirty secular compositions, as well as five Masses and two motets, written over the succeeding sixty or seventy years.[1] The present edition contains all the secular settings of "Fors seulement" that are preserved in complete form, beginning with Ockeghem's original (in two versions, nos. [1a] and [1b]) and extending to a distant relative by Adrian Willaert. This collection of thirty compositions illustrates stylistic change in northern Renaissance music, ranging from the three-part song forms of the fifteenth century to various examples of vocal and instrumental polyphony, treatment of a *cantus firmus*, degrees of partial and pervasive imitation, canon, melodic paraphrase, and parody, as they evolved in the first half of the sixteenth century.

Virtually all the "Fors seulement" pieces are by Netherlanders or Frenchmen; only one German is represented in the collection (see below). Ockeghem himself was probably the first to base a new composition on his own *rondeau*, as he wrote a *Missa Fors seulement* and is named as the composer of a second chanson (see no. [2]). However, most contributors of settings of "Fors seulement" belong to the generation following Ockeghem: these include such outstanding masters as Jacob Obrecht (d. 1505); Anthoine de Févin (d. 1512); Pierre de la Rue (d. 1518); Josquin des Prez (d. 1521); Marbriano de Orto (d. 1529); Antoine Brumel; Antonius Divitis; Johannes Ghisling [Ghiselin]; and Matthaeus Pipelare.[2] Their number also includes some obscure figures: there are compositions by Johannes Agricola;[3] Gilles Reingot; Jacobus Romanus; De la Val; and Jörg Blanckenmüller, the only German. The generation after this one is represented by a smaller group—Elzéar Genet [called Carpentras] (d. 1548), Nicolas Gombert (d. ca. 1556), Adrianus Willaert (d. 1562), Andreas de Sylva, and Philippe Verdelot. Among the composers of this group we might also count an Italian, Costanzo Festa (d. 1545), whose setting of "Fors seulement" has been lost.[4]

By far the most frequently borrowed voice of Ockeghem's chanson is its highest-sounding one, which Ockeghem may have called the "tenor" but which later sources (and the present writer) prefer to label as the "superius" (see nos. [2]-[17] below). One of these settings of the superius of Ockeghem's chanson is for three voices (no. [2]), nine settings are for four voices (nos. [3]-[11]), and six are for five voices (nos. [12]-[17]). Two other compositions (nos. [18] and [19]) are based on the middle voice of Ockeghem's piece, which we shall call the "tenor." An exceptional setting is one by Ghisling (no. [20]) that employs portions of both superius and tenor. Three compositions (nos. [21]-[23]) are based on Ockeghem's contratenor; two of these are for four voices, and one is for five. Late in the fifteenth century a new tenor became associated with themes from Ockeghem's pieces (see nos. [24] and [25] and

Plate IV), and this melody was used as a *cantus firmus* independently of Ockeghem's music in nos. [26] and [27]; thus a second branch of the "Fors seulement" family came into existence. Moreover, in the early sixteenth century, the technique of parody began to supplant *cantus firmus* as a basis for making new music out of old,[5] and the "new" tenor underwent various transformations (nos. [28] and [29]). Finally, the process was ended by Willaert's *cantus firmus* setting based on a parody (no. [30]).

The idea of gathering together many different "Fors seulement" settings goes back to the early sixteenth century. The most extensive collection, containing twelve settings, is a song book originally owned by Fridolin Sicher, the organist of the monastery of St. Gall in Switzerland, and now held by the St. Gall Stiftsbibliothek (MS 461). The manuscript carries the date 1545, but it was probably copied some years earlier.[6] Florence Conservatory, MS B.2439, the so-called "Basevi Codex," is an early sixteenth-century Netherlands manuscript that contains seven four-part settings of "Fors seulement" in succession, as well as a three-part setting elsewhere in the manuscript.[7] Of comparable importance as a source of "Fors seulement" settings is Vienna, Österreichischen Nationalbibliothek, MS 18746. This is a set of five partbooks, copied partly in the hand of the Netherlands court scribe Pierre Alamire and dated 1523, that contains a section devoted to seven five-part settings of Ockeghem's chanson.[8] Finally, an early sixteenth-century German manuscript, the Regensburg, Proske-Bibliothek MS C. 120 (the "Pernner Codex"), contains six successive "Fors seulement" settings.[9] The present edition fulfills these early desires to bring together the shorter works based on Ockeghem's chanson or on one of its derivatives.

For over a century, music historians have regarded the "Fors seulement" series of compositions as a touchstone of Renaissance borrowing practices. The first scholar to attempt to name and describe the compositions of "Fors seulement" was August Wilhelm Ambros (1868), whose list was amplified by Otto Kade in his revision of Ambros's work[10] and further enlarged by Otto Gombosi in his study of Obrecht.[11] Most recently, Helen Hewitt has produced a definitive list of thirty-five "Fors seulement" pieces, exclusive of the Masses.[12] Two of these settings are incomplete,[13] and two others, sacred motets for five voices, stand outside the main body of secular pieces because of their liturgical or ceremonial character.[14] Hewitt excludes from her list the lost work of Costanzo Festa (see above), as well as a piece attributed to "Andreas pleni (?)" that appears to have no musical relationship to other "Fors seulement" pieces.[15] All of the secular settings that survive in complete form are transcribed in the present edition; these include thirteen that have never before been published in modern edition and others that heretofore have been available only in unreliable transcriptions (see the Commentary for each work, below). The purpose of this edition is to provide the means for comparative study and performance of all members of the "Fors seulement" family in a volume that combines scholarly accuracy with practicality.

Texts and Performance Media

As will be discussed in more detail below, there are some members of the "Fors seulement" family that are either untexted or that have only a textual incipit in their sources (e.g., no. [4]). However, where texts are present in the sources, they are reproduced in the edition. Textual variants (see below) are many, and the present edition does not attempt to cite them all. In this edition, the text readings follow the orthography of the principal musical sources unless otherwise noted.

Four different poems appear among the musical compositions in the "Fors seulement" family. Three of these are complete *rondeaux*. The original, and most frequently used, text is the *rondeau cinquain* (i.e., a *rondeau* with a five-line stanza) "Fors seulement l'attente," for which Ockeghem composed a three-part setting (the two versions of which are nos. [1a] and [1b]). This text, with minor variants, is also set in nos. [3], [5], [12], [13], [24], and [26]. A different *rondeau*, "Fors seulement contre ce qu'ay promys," appears in a second setting attributed to Ockeghem (no. [2]). Yet another *rondeau*, "Du tout plongiet au lac de desespoir," appears in one source of a setting by Brumel (no. [6]), in which the "Fors seulement l'attente" text remains associated only with the voice borrowed from Ockeghem's piece. The last text, a parody of the original *rondeau* text, "Fors seulement la mort," is set by Févin (no. [28]) and Willaert (no. [30]). All of these texts are printed below (pp. xxviii–xxx) in their entirety (even though only their refrains are underlaid to the music in the sources).

Just as the various sources transmit variants in the music, so, also, do they reveal textual differences. Many of these differences are merely orthographic (e.g., "Fors seullement" or "Forseulement"), while others involve differences concerning single words, phrases, and, sometimes, whole lines (e.g., line 7 in nos. [1a] and [1b]).

Some settings, including Ockeghem's own (nos. [1a], [1b], and [2]), are clearly designed to be sung as complete *rondeaux* with refrains and two verses (see below for a discussion of form), and thus they feature extensive musical repetition. Other compositions are supplied only with the text of the refrain, or with no text at all, and they appear to abandon the repetition scheme of the *rondeau*. However, if a medial cadence is provided in the music to permit the necessary repetitions, singers may perform all verses of a *rondeau* at their discretion. The text underlay of the refrains can be used for the verses. No source provides underlay for more than the refrain, so this must have been a task routinely assumed by the singers. Performance of a complete *rondeau cinquain* follows the scheme outlined below:

Text	Lines	Music
Refrain	1-3	A
	4-5	B
Verse 1	6-8	A
Refrain	1-3	A
Verse 2	9-11	A
	12-13	B
Refrain	1-3	A
	4-5	B

In many sources, only an incipit serves to identify the text, and the style of the music often suggests instrumental performance. Editorial judgment, based on musical style and on indications appearing in the sources, has been used in determining whether a given setting is likely to be vocal or instrumental. These judgments and the reasons for making them are documented in the commentaries on the affected pieces. The distinction concerning vocal or instrumental performance was rarely made in fifteenth- and early sixteenth-century chansons, and editorial suggestions for performance are offered with due reserve.

Settings without text can be performed instrumentally. Any combination of voices and instruments may be employed for settings supplied with text. Appropriate instruments of the period, such as viols, recorders, and lute, are desirable; but modern wind and string instruments may also be used. Care should be taken to maintain a proper balance in dynamics, however, and vibrato should be kept to a minimum, both in singing and playing. No more than two voices or instruments should be assigned to a part; voices may be supported by a single instrument in unison.

Editorial Principles

The transcription of each piece in this edition is based on a single source, manuscript or printed, selected on the basis of its relative accuracy and on either chronological priority or provenance close to the composer. The choice was often difficult, and sometimes it was arbitrary. Ockeghem's original chanson poses special problems because of the great differences among the various sources. These sources tend to fall into two groups, representing two distinct versions of the work (see the commentary for nos. [1a] and [1b]). Both versions have considerable authority, and there is a possibility that Ockeghem revised the work himself. Therefore, both versions of the original chanson appear in the edition.

Obvious errors and corruptions have been corrected, and the corrections are cited in the Notes to the Transcription section following the commentary on each piece. Textual variants among the voice-parts within a single source have been reconciled without comment. Where texts are omitted in the sources of pieces that, in the editor's opinion, were intended to be sung, underlay has been added in brackets. Reduction of note values is generally in the proportion 2:1 (semibreve = half-note). The only exception to this kind of reduction is in the transcription of the two versions, [1a] and [1b], of Ockeghem's original composition, which reflects an apparently earlier notational practice that requires a 4:1 reduction (semibreve = quarter-note).[16] Final longas of all pieces have been transcribed as breves in the edition in order to convey the idea of an indefinite final note value.

The order of voices in the sources has sometimes been changed to reflect the actual pitch order. Where the voices are designated in the source by such terms as "tenor" or "contra," these terms have been retained in the transcription. However, except for no. [23], where a *quinta vox* part occupies the second line, in the commentary on those pieces that have both a contratenor altus and a contratenor bassus line, the second line of the transcription is referred to as "altus" and the lowest line is referred to as "bassus" (e.g., see commentary on no. [3]).

Ligatures are indicated in the edition by a solid bracket above the notes affected. Coloration is indicated by an open bracket. Coronas (⌒) are used in the transcription to represent similar signs (⌒ or ⅄) that mark medial or final cadences in the sources. The sign of congruence (⅄), indicating the entry of canonic voices, is used in the transcription just as it is used in the sources (e.g., see no. [12]). Accidentals on the staff are those found in the primary source for each piece. Accidentals marking editorial *musica ficta* have been added above the notes in accordance with the generally accepted practices of raising the seventh degree at cadences (or, where the context calls for it, lowering the second degree) and avoiding tritones and other augmented or diminished intervals. In cases where the evidence for *musica ficta* is ambiguous, such as raising the seventh degree at a weak or passing cadence (e.g., no. [3], m. 21), or where it produces a cross-relation with another voice (e.g., no. [17], m. 110), the accidentals are given in parentheses to emphasize their optional character. The signature in the contra of no. [20] is enclosed in parentheses because that signature is not present in the source.

Commentary and Notes

The commentary on each transcription provides a list of sources and modern editions, a reference to the appropriate number in Hewitt's list (see p. viii), a brief description of the work, and critical notes as required. The name of the primary source for each transcription is marked with an asterisk in the source lists. In the commentary for nos. [2]-[30], references to Ockeghem's original piece are to version [1b], unless otherwise noted (see below). The following abbreviations are used in the commentary: Tr. = treble; S. = superius; A. = altus; Ct. = contra(tenor); T. = tenor; B. = bassus; 5ta = *quinta vox*; m. (mm.) = measure (measures); Br. = breve; L. = longa; Sb. = semibreve; M. = minim; Sm. = semiminim; F. = fusa; and fol. (fols.) = folio (folios).

[1a]   [Johannes] O[c]keghem

SOURCES AND EDITIONS
*Dijon, Bibliothèque publique, MS 517, fols. 28'-29, "Okeghem."

Washington, D.C., Library of Congress, M2.1 L25 Case (MS Laborde), fols. 99'-100, anon.

Modern edition: E. Droz, G. Thibault, and Y. Rokseth, eds., *Trois chansonniers français du XVe siècle*, I (Paris, 1927), p. 48 (after Dijon 517).

Hewitt list: No. 1.

COMMENTARY
This version of Ockeghem's piece is written in the same hand in both manuscript sources, and their readings are essentially the same.[17] Dijon and Laborde preserve a chanson repertoire of ca. 1470, and this may be the earlier of the two versions of Ockeghem's work; it lacks many of the dotted rhythms and passing notes of the better-known version (no. [1b]).

A curious feature of no. [1a] is the ambiguity of the sources in distinguishing superius from tenor. The voice on the left-hand page of the source manuscripts, where the superius is normally entered, has a lower range than that on the right, where the tenor normally appears. This lower voice has the descending cadence that is usually associated with the tenor part in fifteenth-century music. Neither voice is identified by name. In this edition, these parts are placed according to their pitch order as in such later sources (for no. [1b]) as Paris 1597, Rome Cappella Giulia XIII.27, and St. Gall 461. In the manuscript sources for no. [1a], the full text is written only under the voice on the left-hand page; however, both upper voices are assumed to carry the text. The complete *rondeau* text is given in the section Texts and Translations.

For the transcription in this edition, note values are in a 4:1 reduction in recognition of the archaic style of this piece. Except for no. [1b], which is also transcribed in 4:1 reduction, a 2:1 reduction applies to all the later settings, including one other with a source-attribution to Ockeghem (no. [2]).

NOTE TO THE TRANSCRIPTION
(1) M. 5, Ct., the e-flat is signed in both the primary source and in the Laborde MS; but it is lacking in all sources of version [1b].

[1b]   [Johannes Ockeghem]

SOURCES AND EDITIONS
Paris, Bibliothèque nationale, fonds français MS 1597, fols. xxxvi'-xxxvii, anon.

Rome, Vatican City, Biblioteca Apostolica Vaticana, Cappella Giulia, MS XIII.27, fols. 104'-105 (97'-98), anon. (incipit: "Frayres y dexedes me").

St. Gall, Stiftsbibliothek, MS 461, pp. 2-3, "Ockenhem."

*Wolfenbüttel, Herzog-August-Bibliothek, MS 287 Extravag., fols. 43'-45, anon.

Modern editions: F. J. Giesbert, ed., *Ein altes Spielbuch: Liber Fridolini Sichery* (Mainz, 1936), p. 2; O. Gombosi, *Jacob Obrecht: Eine stilkritische Studie* (Leipzig, 1925), Anhang, no. IX (both after St. Gall MS 461).

Hewitt list: No. 1.

COMMENTARY
The Wolfenbüttel MS 287, of French or Burgundian origin, dates from ca. 1480 and is the earliest of the sources containing this second version of

Ockeghem's piece.[18] Distinguishing version [1b] from version [1a] are its many groups of dotted semibreves and pairs of semiminims (𝅗𝅥. ♩♩) replacing groups of undotted semibreves and pairs of minims (𝅗𝅥 ♩♩), notably in m. 3 of the tenor (see Ex. 1) and in m. 12 of the superius. This uneven rhythm is adopted in all settings that borrow the "Fors seulement" theme, including Ockeghem's own *Missa Fors seulement*. Because Ockeghem used this rhythm in the Mass, the conclusion is inescapable that version [1b] of the chanson is authentic, although version [1a] may represent an earlier state of the composition.

However, although we have identified no. [1b] as being characterized by dotted values, there is one dotted rhythm in the primary source for [1b] that is probably *not* authentic. This dotted rhythm (see Ex. 3 for the transcription of this rhythm) occurs in the superius at mm. 63:3-64:2 of all sources for no. [1b] except St. Gall 461, an early sixteenth-century manuscript probably of Flemish origin and acquired in 1545 by the Swiss organist Fridolin Sicher. Because the dotted rhythm is reproduced not only in the majority of sources for no. [1b], but also in the sources for some of the "Fors seulement" settings by other composers (e.g., nos. [3], [14], and [15]), this uneven reading has been allowed to stand in the transcription of [1b] given in the present edition. On the other hand, the St. Gall 461 source for [1b] gives an undotted reading in mm. 63-64 (and so, of course, does the basically undotted no. [1a]), and there are many "Fors seulement" settings that show a similarly even rendition of these measures in the superius (see Ex. 2).

As in the manuscript sources for no. [1a], the Wolfenbüttel manuscript places the lower-sounding voice on the left and the higher voice on the right; but Paris, Rome, and St. Gall place the voices in their pitch order, with superius on the left and tenor on the right. The complete *rondeau* text for [1b] is given in the section Texts and Translations.

Ex. 1: transcription of m. 3, T., of no. [1a] (left) and [1b].

Ex. 2: transcription of mm. 63-64, S., as they occur in the sources of no. [1a] and in the St. Gall 461 source of no. [1b].

Ex. 3: transcription of mm. 63-64, S., as they occur in all sources of no. [1b] except St. Gall 461.

NOTES TO THE TRANSCRIPTION

(1) M. 11, S., an extra Sb. appears here in the source.

(2) Mm. 34-35, S. has L. in the source.

(3) Mm. 63:3-64:2, S. has Sb., Sb. in St. Gall 461, as in no. [1a].

[2]   [Johannes] O[c]keghem

SOURCES AND EDITIONS

Copenhagen, Kongelige Bibliotek, Ny Kgl. Saml. MS 1848-2°, p. 427, anon.

Florence, Biblioteca del Conservatorio "L. Cherubini," MS Basevi 2439, fols. lii'-liii, "J. Ockeghem."

Paris, Bibliothèque nationale, fonds français MS 1596, fols. 7'-8, anon.

*Paris, Bibliothèque nationale, fonds français MS 2245, fols. 16'-17, "Okeghem."

St. Gall, Stiftsbibliothek, MS 461, pp. 4-5, "Ockengem."

Trium vocum carmina (Nuremberg: H. Formschneider, 1538), no. 47, anon.

Modern editions: Giesbert, *Ein altes Spielbuch*, p. 4 (after St. Gall); Gombosi, *Jacob Obrecht*, Anhang, no. X (after Florence).

Hewitt list: No. 14.

COMMENTARY

Paris MS 2245 bears the arms of the Duke of Orléans, the future Louis XII (reigned 1498-1515).[19] An almost (one line is inadvertently omitted) complete "new" *rondeau* text, "Fors seulement contre ce qu'ay promys," is provided for the two upper voices. The rubric "Canon/Royal" in Paris MS 2245 may refer to the transposition of the contra a twelfth below the notated pitch; the Duke of Orléans's anticipated title as Louis XII could have suggested such a transposition and the rubric indicating it.

Gombosi doubts Ockeghem's authorship on stylistic grounds.[20] (To the clumsy and uncharacteristic passages that Gombosi cites might be added the exposed fifths in m. 17.) Nevertheless, three generally reliable sources name Ockeghem as the composer. The relatively early date of Paris MS 2245 (before 1498), as well as the persistent independence of the voices, which avoid the slightest hint of imitation, suggest that this may be the earliest in the long line of chanson settings based on Ockeghem's original composition. Here the original superius is transposed down to become the contra.

The "new" *rondeau* text ("Fors seullement contre ce qu'ay promys") is found both in the primary source and in the contemporary MS Paris 1596. Florence 2439, on the other hand, supplies only the original text, "Fors seullement l'attente." The remaining sources limit the text incipit to "Fors seulement." The new text may have been added to a pre-existent piece; it contains veiled political references that suggest the hand of the Duke himself, who as son of Charles d'Orléans may have inherited some of his father's literary talent. The complete *rondeau* text is given in the section Texts and Translations.

NOTES TO THE TRANSCRIPTION

(1) Ct. = S. of no. [1b] transposed down a 12th. In Paris MS 2245 the borrowed voice is notated at its original pitch, and the transposition is suggested, somewhat vaguely, by the rubric "Canon/Royal" before and above the initial letter "F" of the S. text. (The word "Canon" appears before the initial letter, and the word "Royal" appears above the initial letter.) In all other sources the transposition is fully written out.

(2) In St. Gall 461 a measure is inserted before m. 1 to give the T. the rhythm of no. [1a-b] (Br., Sb., Sb.), while the S. and Ct. begin with L. rather than Br. In Florence 2439 the S. and Ct. are unchanged, but the T. of m. 1 has the rhythm Sb., M., M. Both variants appear to be efforts to clarify the imitation and are not likely to have been part of the original composition. Copenhagen 1848 and Paris 1596 have the same reading of the opening as Paris 2245.

(3) M. 24, S., and M. 30, Ct., Coronas appear here in the source, apparently in error. The proper medial cadence of the *rondeau* is in m. 38.

(4) M. 63, the final note of the Ct. does not appear in the source, which quotes the borrowed melody literally. This note is provided in the other sources, which also present the melody transposed.

[3] [Jacob] Hobrecht

SOURCES AND EDITIONS

*Florence, Biblioteca del Conservatorio "L. Cherubini," MS Basevi 2439, fols. xxiii'-xxiiii, "Hobrecht."

Regensburg, Proske-Bibliothek, MS C. 120 (Pernner Codex), pp. 320-323, "Hobrecht."

St. Gall, Stiftsbibliothek, MS 461, pp. 12-13, "Obrecht."

Canti C (Venice: O. Petrucci, 1504), fols. 4'-5, "Ja. Obreht."

Modern editions: J. Obrecht, *Werken*, ed. J. Wolf, VII: *Wereldlijke Werken* (Amsterdam, s.d.), p. 14; A. W. Ambros, *Geschichte der Musik*, V (Leipzig, 1911): 29 (after *Canti C*); Giesbert, *Ein altes Spielbuch*, p. 12 (after St. Gall 461).

Hewitt list: No. 4.

COMMENTARY

Ockeghem's superius, transposed down a fourth, serves as Obrecht's altus ("contra"). In mm. 63-64, the dotted variant (see above, Ex. 3) of this voice is used. No source provides the full text, but a medial cadence is specified, and performance as a *rondeau* is thereby implied. The refrain text has been underlaid in this edition to make this option possible.

Obrecht adheres closely to Ockeghem's themes, while expanding his contrapuntal design by introducing imitation at the opening (*a* 4), in mm. 43 ff. (*a* 3) and again in mm. 60 ff. (*a* 4).

NOTES TO THE TRANSCRIPTION

(1) Incipit, S., the f-flat appearing here is present in the source; it means that the F is "*ficta*," or outside the Guidonian gamut.

(2) M. 42, B., the source has Sb., Sb., with a *signum congruentiae* over the first of these; this sign, which marks the medial cadence, has been moved by the editor to the Sb. in the preceding measure, to correspond with the S. and T.; in all other sources the Br. in m. 42 is a L.

[4] [Pierre de la] Rue

SOURCES AND EDITIONS

*Florence, Biblioteca del Conservatorio "L. Cherubini," MS Basevi 2439, fols. xviiii'-xx, "Rue."

Regensburg, Proske-Bibliothek, MS C. 120 (Pernner Codex), pp. 326-327, "P. De *la* Rue" (the syllable *la* is written as a musical note).

St. Gall, Stiftsbibliothek, MS 461, pp. 14-15, "Pirson."

Modern edition: Giesbert, *Ein altes Spielbuch*, p. 14 (after St. Gall 461).

Hewitt list: No. 5.

COMMENTARY

The Florence manuscript is a major Netherlands source for la Rue's secular works.[21] No medial cadence is indicated, and only incipits of the text are provided. Thus, instrumental performance is probably intended.

The superius of Ockeghem's piece [1b], transposed down a fifth, serves as the altus ("contra") in la Rue's setting, with the nine introductory measures of rest being reduced to two. In all sources, mm. 56-57 of the altus have the undotted variant of Ockeghem's superius (see Ex. 2), although this produces an eleventh with the bass. The temptation to substitute the dotted variant, which would be consonant, should be avoided because such dissonance is consistent with la Rue's style. (Note the dissonant f in the T., m. 8, also given in all sources.)

La Rue begins his setting with a syncopated motive in imitation, to which he returns in mm. 46 ff. Rhythmically similar motives appear with insistent regularity (mm. 19 ff., 27 ff.) so that the entire piece is permeated by them, relegating Ockeghem's voice to an aurally subordinate role. For another setting by la Rue of this *cantus firmus*, see no. [12] below.

[5]   [Matthaeus] Pipelare

SOURCE AND EDITION

*Florence, Biblioteca del Conservatorio "L. Cherubini," MS Basevi 2439, fols. xxi'-xxii, "Pipelare."

Modern edition: M. Pipelare, *Opera omnia*, ed. R. Cross (American Institute of Musicology, 1966-67), I: 9.

Hewitt list: No. 8.

COMMENTARY

In this setting for low voices, Ockeghem's superius, transposed down an octave, serves as altus ("cont."). Pipelare has added a breve-rest to Ockeghem's original nine breve-rests at the beginning of the piece in the altus. The first ten measures of Ockeghem's tenor are reproduced in the tenor of Pipelare's setting. In general, Pipelare adopted Ockeghem's melodic ideas as the basis for his piece, extending them through imitation and complementary counterpoints. Though the full text is not supplied, and no medial cadence is indicated, the supple melodic style, close to Ockeghem's own, suggests vocal performance, and the editor has underlaid the refrain text as used in nos. [1a] and [1b].

NOTE TO THE TRANSCRIPTION

(1) M. 42, A. ("cont."), Florence 2439 has a Br.-rest. In Ockeghem's superius the final L. of the *prima pars* is dotted and the *secunda pars* opens with five Br. of rest. Extension of the previous L. is desirable in this measure, and no reason for altering Ockeghem's voice is apparent. We have therefore restored Ockeghem's reading in this measure.

[6]   [Antoine Brumel]

SOURCES AND EDITIONS

*Brussels, Bibliothèque royale, MS 228, fols. 18'-19, anon.

Florence, Biblioteca del Conservatorio "L. Cherubini," MS Basevi 2439, fols. xx'-xxi, "Brumel."

Munich, Bayerische Staatsbibliothek, Mus. MS 1516, no. 2, anon. (a 5th higher; copied from *Canti C*?).

Regensburg, Proske-Bibliothek, MS C. 120 (Pernner Codex), pp. 324-325, "An. Brumel."

St. Gall, Stiftsbibliothek, MS 461, pp. 16-17, "Brumel."

Canti C (Venice: O. Petrucci, 1504), fols. 5'-6, "Alexander" (a 5th higher).

Modern editions: A. Brumel, *Opera omnia*, ed. B. Hudson (American Institute of Musicology, 1972), VI: 74; A. Agricola, *Opera omnia*, ed. E. R. Lerner (American Institute of Musicology, 1970), V: 124, as doubtful work of Agricola; M. Picker, ed., *The Chanson Albums of Marguerite of Austria* (Berkeley, 1965), p. 237 (after Brussels MS 228); R.-J. van Maldeghem, ed., *Trésor musical, Musique profane*, XXI (Brussels, 1885): 27, attributed to Pierre de la Rue (after Brussels MS 228); J. Obrecht, *Werken*, ed. J. Wolf, VII: *Wereldlijke Werken* (Amsterdam, s.d.), p. 85 (after Regensburg MS C. 120); Giesbert, *Ein altes Spielbuch*, p. 16 (after St. Gall 461).

Hewitt list: No. 6.

COMMENTARY

Brussels MS 228 was written ca. 1525 for Margaret of Austria, regent of the Netherlands. This is the only source containing the unusual text underlaid to no. [6]; even Florence MS 2439, which is closely related to the Brussels manuscript in origin and content, lacks this poem. It may, therefore, have been added to suit the taste of Margaret; on the other hand, because the low register and unusual transposition of the *cantus firmus* appear to symbolize the opening words, "Plunged into the lake of despair," the poem may well have been the original text of Brumel's setting.[22]

The voice marked "tenor" (altus) presents the superius of Ockeghem's piece transposed down a major ninth, with the necessary signature of two flats. Actually, in this setting for low voices, this transposed part lies somewhat higher than the "contra" (tenor). Therefore, the inner voices have been exchanged in the transcription in this edition to clarify this relationship.

Brumel omits the opening rests of Ockeghem's *cantus firmus*, and begins his setting in solemn homophony. The presence of a complete *rondeau* text, together with the apparently symbolic character of the music, indicates vocal performance. The lowest notes in the Baricanor (bass) at measures 2 and 62 may be outside the range of the available voices or instruments. Thus, at m. 62, the Brussels manuscript provides an alternative note an octave higher; and the Florence and St. Gall manuscripts give alternative pitches an octave above both in measures 2 and 62. The complete *rondeau* text is given in the section Texts and Translations.

[7]   G[illes] Reingot

Source

Canti C (Venice: O. Petrucci, 1504), fols. 23'-25, "G. Reingot."

Hewitt list: No. 13.

Commentary

The composer of this setting, Gilles Reingot, was an obscure member of the chapel of Charles V.[23] In his piece, Ockeghem's superius, transposed down an octave, serves as tenor, while the first ten measures of Ockeghem's tenor appear in Reingot's superius. Around these quoted melodies Reingot has woven lively, intricate lines of markedly instrumental design.

[8]   [Marbriano] de Orto

Source

*Florence, Biblioteca del Conservatorio "L. Cherubini," MS Basevi 2439, fols. xxii'-xxiii, "De orto."

Hewitt list: No. 16.

Commentary

Ockeghem's superius, transposed down a twelfth, serves as bassus here, with the introductory rests of the model reduced by one breve, the dotted long concluding the *prima pars* reduced to one breve (m. 38), and the rests opening the *secunda pars* extended by one breve (mm. 39-44). The penultimate note (g) in the bassus was added to Ockeghem's original by de Orto (the final bracketed breve has been added editorially in order to sustain the note through the final measure). The first nine measures of Ockeghem's tenor, transposed up a fourth, open the piece in the superius; the motive presented by these measures is imitated in diminution by the altus ("contra"). Although Ockeghem's melody is again anticipated by imitation in mm. 36 ff., de Orto generally develops his own motives in an instrumental manner. He shows his customary attention to harmonic color, calling frequently for e-flat and specifying sharps in mm. 9 and 17, and even in Ockeghem's *cantus firmus* in m. 26.[24]

Note to the Transcription

(1) M. 35, A. ("contra"), in Florence 2439, the words "Qui n'est dolour" appear here. They may be intended to signal the appearance of the theme of the *secunda pars* in m. 36, overlapping the conclusion of the *prima pars* in the B. two measures later. It is unlikely that de Orto intended vocal performance.

[9]   Jo[hannes] Agricola

Source and Edition

*St. Gall, Stiftsbibliothek MS 461, pp. 18-19, "Jo. Agricola."

Modern edition: Giesbert, *Ein altes Spielbuch*, p. 18.

Hewitt list: No. 15.

Commentary

Ockeghem's superius, transposed down a twelfth, serves as Agricola's bassus. Ockeghem's opening rests are omitted in this setting, and the dotted longa that concludes the *prima pars* is reduced here to a simple longa (mm. 30-31). Moreover, a concluding note, g, has been added by the composer for the final cadence in this setting, much as in de Orto's work (no. [8]). In the final measure of no. [9], the altus has both the third and fifth of the final chord, perhaps as alternatives or as an actual *divisi*. No medial cadence is provided, and the style is decidedly instrumental.

The identity of the composer of no. [9] remains open to question. The manuscript names "Jo." (presumably Johannes) Agricola, an otherwise unknown composer.[25] Famous, however, was Alexander Agricola, whose angular melodic style, unsettled rhythms, and taste for dissonance all appear to be reflected in this piece. Edward Lerner does not include this setting in his edition of Alexander Agricola's *Opera omnia* (American Institute of Musicology, 1961–), and, in fact, this piece is not up to Alexander's customary high level of workmanship. The ninth between superius and tenor at the beginning of m. 33 is one of many awkward spots.

[10]   [Anonymous]

Source and Edition

*St. Gall, Stiftsbibliothek, MS 461, pp. 20-21.

Modern edition: Giesbert, *Ein altes Spielbuch*, p. 20.

Hewitt list: No. 17.

Commentary

Ockeghem's superius, transposed down a twelfth, serves as the bassus in this work. The opening rests of the model are omitted, and a final g is added by the composer of this work (as in the settings of de Orto and Agricola). The altus presents

Ockeghem's theme in diminution, while the tenor and superius ("discantus") offer a counter-theme that bears some resemblance to Ockeghem's second setting (no. [2]). Reference to Ockeghem's original melody is again made, in all voices, at mm. 33 ff. A medial cadence is hinted at in m. 33; but the style seems unsuited to vocal performance, and, thus, text has not been added in the transcription.

[11] Andreas de Sylva

Source

*Bologna, Civico Museo Bibliografico Musicale, MS Q 19, fols. 2'-3, "Andreas de Sylva."

Hewitt list: No. 3.

Commentary

In this unusual setting for four basses ("ad aequales," or for voices in approximately the same register), the part assigned the position of "superius" is Ockeghem's superius, transposed down a twelfth, with its opening rests omitted. De Sylva's setting is interesting regarding *musica ficta* because he uses explicit sharps, creating major thirds, even in the *cantus firmus* (m. 18), and even though this usage leads to a cross-relation with the tenor (m. 19). The source manuscript, of north Italian provenance, is dated 1518 and is a major source for Italo-French music.[26] Concerning the shadowy de Sylva (or Silva), virtually all that is certain is that he was in the service of Pope Leo X in Rome in 1519.[27] The wide ranges of the voices and their long, irregular phrases suggest that this work was designed for instrumental performance.

[12] [Pierre de la] Rue

Source and Edition

*Vienna, Österreichische Nationalbibliothek, MS 18746, No. 56, "Rue" (the S., A., and B. are copied twice).

Modern edition: Gombosi, *Jacob Obrecht*, Anhang, no. XIII.

Hewitt list: No. 2.

Commentary

The unique source for this setting is a manuscript signed by the Netherlands court scribe Pierre Alamire, and dated 1523.[28] This manuscript is related to both Brussels 228 and Florence 2439, which also contain a number of "Fors seulement" compositions.[29] It is, moreover, a central source for those works that la Rue composed for the Hapsburg-Burgundian court.

Ockeghem's superius is taken over without change by la Rue, who also reproduces the first seven measures of Ockeghem's tenor in the bassus of his setting, and adds a *quinta vox* in canon at the fifth with the bassus. Here and in nos. [14], [15], [16], and [23], the *quinta vox* or 5ta appears in a partbook labeled Secundus Tenor in the sources. The piece is divided into two *partes*, indicating that vocal performance as a *rondeau* is intended, even though the manuscript lacks text. In the present edition, the refrain text (that of nos. [1a] and [1b]) has been underlaid to the music.

When la Rue's four-part setting (no. [4]) is compared with this work, we see that no. [12] is conceived in a more vocal style that gives Ockeghem's melody greater prominence. It is, nevertheless, an intricately contrapuntal work, with strongly marked dissonances and syncopations.

Notes to the Transcription

(1) 5ta part is given in a partbook labeled Secundus Tenor in the source, where this voice which is in canon with the B. at the 5th, is fully written out, including its deviation from the B. in m. 26.

(2) Mm. 28-44, T. is written a third too low in the source.

[13] [Anonymous]

Sources

St. Gall, Stiftsbibliothek, MS 463, no. 194 (S., A., 5ta) ("Fors seulement . . . Secundum," "Dorius i. Primus").

St. Gall, Stiftsbibliothek, MS 464, fol. 9' (S. B.).

*Vienna, Österreichische Nationalbibliothek, MS 18746, no. 51.

Hewitt list: No. 10.

Commentary

A few errors in the Vienna manuscript are corrected in accord with the St. Gall manuscripts, as noted. Though fragmentary, these St. Gall manuscripts are of unusual interest. They were owned by, and MS 463 was copied by, the Swiss humanist Aegidius Tschudi (1505-1572), who was a student of the eminent theorist Heinrich Glareanus.[30] Tschudi assigned the pieces in these manuscripts to modes according to the twelve-mode system of Glareanus; no. [13] is unmistakably in the first (Dorian) mode despite its conclusion in a half-cadence on A.

Ockeghem's superius serves here as altus; its transposition an octave lower is suggested by the verbal "canon" inscribed in the margin: "Whoever rises higher than he ought, falls farther than he would wish." Ockeghem's tenor is quoted by the superius in the first ten measures of this setting. The emphatic medial cadence, relatively short phrases, and frequent repeated notes imply vocal performance. The refrain text (after that of nos. [1a] and [1b]) has been underlaid here by the editor.

NOTES TO THE TRANSCRIPTION

(1) A. = S. of no. [1] transposed down an octave. It is notated at the original pitch, the transcription being indicated by the following rubric: "Canon: Qui plus hault monte qui ne doit / De plus hault chet qui ne vouldroit." The A. is contained in the Secundus Tenor partbook in the source, while the 5ta is given in the A. book; these parts have been exchanged in the transcription in order to reflect their actual pitch relationship.

(2) M. 35, A., notes 1 and 2 represented by Br. in the source; division into Sb. Sb. is required by text underlay.

(3) Mm. 60-61, 5ta, note 3 of m. 60 and note 1 of m. 61 represented by Br. in the source; division is required by the text underlay.

(4) Mm. 68-69, B., notes 2-3 of m. 68 and note 1 of m. 69 have rhythm of dotted Sb., M., Sb., making fifths with the A. in the source. The reading in this edition is from St. Gall 464.

(5) M. 69, A., note 2, source has colored M., in error, for colored Sb.

(6) M. 79: 3-m. 82, S., source has rhythm Sb., L. (a', a') occupying these mm.; the more interesting reading given here is from the St. Gall MSS.

[14] [Anonymous]

SOURCE

*Vienna, Osterreichische Nationalbibliothek, MS 18746, no. 55.

Hewitt list: No. 9.

COMMENTARY

Ockeghem's superius, transposed down an octave, serves as altus in this piece. However, in this setting, the initial rests in both *partes* of the model are omitted. In m. 48 of the altus the dotted variant (see Ex. 3) is used. Despite the medial cadence, the four newly composed voices of no. [14] maintain such independence from the borrowed voice (i.e., the altus), that the *rondeau* text can be applied only with difficulty. It is possible that the altus is meant to be sung, while the other voices are designed for instruments. In the present edition, therefore, only the altus has been underlaid with text (this text is the same as that for nos. [1a] and [1b]).

NOTES TO THE TRANSCRIPTION

(1) 5ta appears in a partbook labeled Secundus Tenor in the source.

(2) M. 24, A., notes 1 and 2 represented by Br. in the source; division into Sb. Sb. is required by text underlay.

(3) M. 51, T., a c' (M.) is inserted between notes 1 and 2 in the source; this must be an error, and it has been omitted in the transcription.

[15] [Anonymous]

SOURCE

*Vienna, Osterreichische Nationalbibliothek, MS 18746, no. 52.

Hewitt list: No. 18.

COMMENTARY

Ockeghem's superius, transposed down a twelfth and with its opening rests omitted, serves as *quinta vox* ("[5ta]") in this setting. From a functional point of view, this *quinta vox* (as well as the [5ta] in no. [16]) is really a "tenor," in that it carries Ockeghem's *cantus firmus*. This 5ta part appears in a partbook labeled Secundus Tenor in the source. In m. 55 of the *quinta vox*, the dotted variant of Ockeghem's superius (see Ex. 3) is used. No medial cadence is provided, and instrumental performance is suggested.

NOTE TO THE TRANSCRIPTION

(1) Mm. 56:3-57:1, 5ta, rhythm is M. Sb. in the source; this edition conforms to Ockeghem and to the imitative pattern.

[16] [Anonymous]

SOURCE

*Vienna, Osterreichische Nationalbibliothek MS 18746, no. 54.

Hewitt list: No. 19.

COMMENTARY

This is one of the most unusual of all the settings. Ockeghem's superius provides the basis for the *quinta vox* ("[5ta]") in this setting, but here the model has been subjected to many alterations. It is transposed down a thirteenth, without flats being added to the signature, thus changing its mode from Aeolian (i.e., minor) to Ionian (i.e., major). (The setting itself begins in the Dorian and ends in the Aeolian mode, quite independently of its *cantus firmus*.) The opening measures of rest are expanded in the setting from the original nine to eleven, and, more unusually, rests are interpolated at mm. 23-24 of no. [16]. One measure of rest in Ockeghem's superius is expanded in the *quinta vox* in this setting to ten at mm. 34-43. The dotted longa concluding the *prima pars* of the model is reduced to a breve (m. 52) here, but the succeeding five measures of rest are enlarged to eight. Eight measures of rest are interpolated at mm. 69-76, and two more measures of rest occur at mm. 83-84. The final longa becomes a breve (m. 94), followed by four measures of rest and a new final note, e. The *quinta vox* appears in a partbook labeled Secundus Tenor in the source.

The first seven measures of the superius and altus in this piece reproduce Ockeghem's tenor and contratenor at their original pitches. The ending of no. [16], which restores the original mode of Ockeghem's piece, is devised by placing the conclusion of Ockeghem's superius, untransposed, in the superius of the new setting. No text is provided in the source, and instrumental performance is recommended.

[17] Antonius Divitis

SOURCE
*Bologna, Civico Museo Bibliografico Musicale, MS Q 19, fols. 9'-11.

Hewitt list: No. 7.

COMMENTARY
Ockeghem's superius, transposed down a fifth and augmented in the proportion 2:1, serves as the altus in this composition. The augmentation is indicated by the mensuration: the source gives C in the altus and ₵ in all the other voices. All rests of a breve or more in Ockeghem's model have been suppressed in the setting, resulting in a work that is somewhat less than double the length of Ockeghem's. The original text, in corrupt form, is underlaid to the altus in the source for no. [17]. However, because of the augmentation, it is unlikely that vocal performance was intended, and so this text has been omitted from the transcription.

Divitis (Le Riche, Rycke) was a Flemish composer notable for his Masses and motets. No. [17] appears to be his only secular work.[31]

NOTES TO THE TRANSCRIPTION
(1) A. = S. of no. [1], transposed down a fifth and augmented 2:1. The full text of the refrain is underlaid to this voice, but is corrupt ("Fours seullement l'etente que ie meur . . . "). It has been omitted from the transcription.

(2) S., T., 5ta, and B. have the corrupt incipit "Fours seullement."

[18] Jacob[us] Roman[us]

SOURCE AND EDITION
*St. Gall, Stiftsbibliothek, MS 461, pp. 24-25, "Jacob' roman."

Modern edition: Giesbert, *Ein altes Spielbuch*, p. 24.

Hewitt list: No. 23.

COMMENTARY
Ockeghem's tenor serves as superius in no. [18]. The first fourteen measures of the setting present Ockeghem's melody canonically at the fourth in the superius and altus voices. At the beginning of the *secunda pars* in this setting, the first two measures of Ockeghem's contra are presented in the bassus (mm. 42-43). The altus of no. [18] at m. 47 reproduces the entry of Ockeghem's superius.

The relatively simple melodic style of the piece suggests vocal performance, and the medial cadence implies *rondeau* form. However, no text is present in the source, and the familiar text does not fit the newly composed voices very convincingly. Therefore this edition provides text (using that of nos. [1a] and [1b]) for the superius only.

The composer's name as given in the source manuscript can be read in various ways (e.g., "Tomman," "Comman," etc.). The most obvious reading, "Romanus," appears in this edition, but the composer's identity remains uncertain.

NOTE TO THE TRANSCRIPTION
(1) M. 62, S., note 1 is c' in St. Gall 461. This reading follows Ockeghem's T.

[19] De la Val

SOURCES AND EDITION
*Regensburg, Proske-Bibliothek, MS C.120 (Pernner Codex), pp. 328-331, "De la Val et Jo."

St. Gall, Stiftsbibliothek, MS 461, pp. 22-23, anon.

Modern edition: Giesbert, *Ein altes Spielbuch*, p. 22 (after St. Gall).

Hewitt list: No. 22.

COMMENTARY
The Regensburg manuscript gives the composer's name as "De la Val et Jo." While the identity of "De la Val" is unknown, "Jo." may well be Johannes Ockeghem, the tenor of whose chanson provides the tenor for De la Val's composition. A few changes, largely of a rhythmic nature, are introduced into this voice, notably at mm. 32-33, 41-42, 59-60, and 64-66 of the setting.

The three newly composed voices in De la Val's setting do not employ themes from Ockeghem, but treat their own motives in a manner similar to la Rue's setting in no. [4]. Indeed, De la Val seems to make conscious use of la Rue's principal motive at mm. 48-52 of no. [19]. The voices lie in a relatively high register (the ranges are Tr., S., A., T.). The medial cadence is ignored, and there is no reflection of textual rhythm or structure in the music. Instrumental performance is therefore suggested.

NOTE TO THE TRANSCRIPTION

(1) M. 42, T., note 1 is d' in the source. The reading in this edition corresponds to St. Gall 461 and to Ockeghem's original.

[20] [Johannes] Ghisling [Verbonet]

SOURCES AND EDITIONS

*Florence, Biblioteca del Conservatorio "L. Cherubini," MS Basevi 2439, fols. xvii'-xviii, "Ghisling."

Regensburg, Proske-Bibliothek, MS C. 120 (Pernner Codex), pp. 332-335, "Verbonet."

Rome, Biblioteca Apostolica, Vaticana, Codicetto Vat. lat. 11953 (B. partbook only), fols. 13-14, anon. (notated a 5th lower).

St. Gall, Stiftsbibliothek, MS 461, pp. 10-11, "Verbonet."

Canti C (Venice: O. Petrucci, 1504), fols. 37'-39, "Ghiselin."

Modern editions: Johannes Ghiselin-Verbonnet, Opera omnia, ed. Clytus Gottwald (American Institute of Musicology, 1968), IV: 8; Giesbert, Ein altes Spielbuch, p. 10 (after St. Gall); Gombosi, Jacob Obrecht, Anhang, no. XI (after Canti C).

Hewitt list: No. 20.

COMMENTARY

This work by the Flemish master Johannes Ghisling (Ghiselin, *alias* Verbonet) is unique among settings of "Fors seulement" in its choice of *cantus firmus*. Its altus ("contra") consists of the first half of Ockeghem's tenor (mm. 1-43) and the second half of his superius (mm. 44-75). The two opening measures of Ockeghem's theme are condensed into one and stated imitatively by all four voices of no. [20], but this opening in the altus is preceded by three measures of rest to permit anticipatory imitation in the other voices. The piece contains a good deal of sequential imitation, much of which is based on Ockeghem's motives. Like no. [19], this setting is written for high voices (ranges are Tr., S., A., T.) and has a generally instrumental aspect. The Florence manuscript is the only source that attributes both nos. [20] and [21] to "Ghisling" and that presents these two settings in succession.

NOTES TO THE TRANSCRIPTION

(1) Incipit, S., the f-flat appearing here is present in the source; it means that the F is *"ficta,"* or outside the Guidonian gamut.

(2) M. 1, Ct., the flat in the signature is not present in the source.

[21] [Incertus]

SOURCES AND EDITIONS

Florence, Biblioteca del Conservatorio "L. Cherubini," MS Basevi 2439, fols. xviii'-xviiii, "Ghisling."

*St. Gall, Stiftsbibliothek, MS 461, pp. 6-7, "Josqin deprecz."

Canti C (Venice: O. Petrucci, 1504), fols. 51'-52, anon.

Modern editions: Johannes Ghiselin-Verbonnet, Opera omnia, ed. Clytus Gottwald (American Institute of Musicology, 1968), IV: 11; Giesbert, Ein altes Spielbuch, p. 6 (after St. Gall); Gombosi, Jacob Obrecht, Anhang, no. XII (after Canti C).

Hewitt list: No. 26.

COMMENTARY

The Florence manuscript, generally a reliable source, is unusually corrupt in its transmission of this work. Its attribution to "Ghisling" is therefore suspect, and it is doubted by both Gombosi[32] and Gottwald.[33] On the other hand, the attribution to Josquin des Prez in the St. Gall manuscript is unconvincing on stylistic grounds. In his monograph on Josquin, Helmuth Osthoff relegates this work to his list of "Doubtful and Inauthentic Compositions."[34]

Ockeghem's contratenor is transposed up an octave and serves as altus for this setting. As in no. [20], the bassus and tenor of this work begin with a condensation of Ockeghem's tenor theme, prefacing a longer quotation of Ockeghem's tenor in the superius (mm. 3-10). No. [21] also shares with no. [20] a predilection for dotted and syncopated motives, as well as the "under-sixth" cadence, which became less common around 1500. On the other hand, no. [21] does not match the clear minor tonality of no. [20]; rather, it vacillates between the transposed Phrygian and Aeolian modes, with frequent inflection of b-flat and b-natural. (Comparison should also be made with no. [22], which has been attributed to Josquin.) The wide ranges of the voices and high level of rhythmic activity imply instrumental performance.

NOTE TO THE TRANSCRIPTION

(1) M. 20, T., note 2 is g in the source. The correct reading is found in Canti C.

[22] [Josquin des Prez?]

SOURCES

*Augsburg, Staats-, Kreis- und Stadtbibliothek, MS 142ª, fols. 40'-42, anon.

Florence, Biblioteca Nazionale Centrale, MS Magl. XIX.164-167, no. LX, anon.

Hewitt list: No. 25.

COMMENTARY

The Augsburg manuscript, the primary source for no. [22], is a compilation of German origin, whose pieces bear various dates from 1499 to 1513. Ockeghem's contratenor, transposed up a fifth, serves as altus for this setting. The transposition is not indicated in the Augsburg source, but it is clearly called for in the concordant Florence manuscript by the word "Canon" and a *custos* at the proper starting pitch, e. The superius of no. [22] reproduces Ockeghem's initial nine measures of rest and the first four measures of his superius melody.

The editorial attribution of this work to Josquin was suggested by the presence of the piece in the midst of a group of five compositions in the Augsburg manuscript that are certainly by Josquin.[35] The intricate manipulation in this piece of forceful rhythmic motives, some derived from Ockeghem and some original, also points to Josquin. The work builds strongly to the final cadence around a dominant pedal in the altus. In m. 40, there appears a version of Ockeghem's contratenor as it occurs in St. Gall 461, where the third quarter-note corresponds to a instead of f; this variant is not found in the major French sources of Ockeghem's piece. (This occurs in no. [23], also.)

The Florence manuscript, an Italian source probably somewhat later in date than the Augsburg one, contains a full refrain text in all voices of this setting. Application of this text is questionable, however; thus the piece is left here without text, just as it is found in Augsburg, and instrumental performance is suggested.

As noted above, Josquin is named in the St. Gall manuscript as composer for no. [21], which is based on the same *cantus firmus* (i.e., Ockeghem's contratenor). It is possible that this ascription to Josquin was an error by the scribe, as he confused the two settings. Josquin is also named as composer of yet another "Fors seulement" setting: Bologna, Civico Museo Bibliografico Musicale, MS R.142, fol. 57', "a sei" (i.e., for 6 voices), of which only the tenor partbook survives. This partbook actually contains only an unaltered statement of Ockeghem's superius (Hewitt No. 11). Thus, no "Fors seulement" setting can be attributed to Josquin with certainty, although there are four possible candidates for this distinction (including no. [23]; see below). Of these four, no. [22] is the one for which the strongest case can be made.

NOTES TO THE TRANSCRIPTION

(1) M. 31, S., note 1 is a dotted Sb. and there is no rest in either the source or the Florence MS. However, because this results in a stylistically unacceptable unresolved 4th, an error must be assumed.

(2) M. 46, note 3-m. 47, B., rhythm is Sb. Br.; Florence MS has Sb. Sb. Sb. (f f e). The transcription here is taken from the Florence MS.

(3) M. 54, B., note 2 is C in the source. The A, given in the Florence MS, is preferable and has been adopted in the transcription.

[23] [Anonymous]

SOURCE
*Vienna, Osterreichische Nationalbibliothek, MS 18746, no. 53

Hewitt list: No. 27.

COMMENTARY

Ockeghem's contratenor serves here as altus, its transposition an octave higher than notated being indicated by a verbal "canon." A similar device is employed in the Florence concordance for no. [22].

A relationship with no. [22] appears in other aspects of this setting, as well. The variant of Ockeghem's contratenor employed in m. 40 of no. [22] occurs in m. 40 of no. [23], also. The rising third motive that plays so important a role throughout this piece in a variety of rhythmic guises may have been suggested by the similar motive that appears in the bassus of no. [22] at mm. 10-13 and reappears in that work in mm. 55-56. (The ultimate source for this motive, of course, is Ockeghem's contratenor, but its particular melodic and rhythmic shape is unique to these two settings.) A pedal-point resulting from the extension of the final note of Ockeghem's contratenor closes both pieces (i.e., nos. [22] and [23]). This densely contrapuntal and richly harmonic chanson is indebted to the four-part setting (no. [22]) that has been attributed to Josquin. Like no. [22], it is best served by instrumental performance to bring out its lively interplay of motives against the placid motion of Ockeghem's contratenor. Indeed, the chain of evidence, weak and circumstantial though it is, suggests that this setting, too, may be a work of Josquin. The importance of the Vienna manuscript (a Netherlands court manuscript dated 1523) as a source for Josquin's and la Rue's late chansons has long been recognized.[36]

NOTES TO THE TRANSCRIPTION

(1) 5ta, this part appears in a Secundus Tenor partbook in the source.

(2) M. 62, B., note 2 is a Sb. in the source.

[24] [Anonymous]

Sources and Edition
*London, British Library, Add. MS 35087, fols. 80'-81.

Chansons a troys (Venice: A. Antico & L. A. Giunta, 1520), fols. 10'-11, 60-60' (T. lacking).

Trium vocum carmina (Nuremberg: H. Formschneider, 1538), no. 46 (notated a 5th lower).

Modern edition: M. Picker, ed., *The Chanson Albums of Marguerite of Austria* (Berkeley, 1965), p. 477.

Hewitt list: No. 29.

Commentary

The first nine measures of the superius in this setting paraphrase Ockeghem's contratenor. When the tenor enters in m. 9 of no. [24], it does not state one of the voices of Ockeghem's chanson, as might be expected. Rather, it carries an entirely new melody that is so well integrated into this setting that we may suspect it to be original, and modeled on Ockeghem's superius only to the extent that its entry is delayed. Because this "new" melody serves as a *cantus firmus* in settings nos. [25]-[27], as well as in Verdelot's motet *Infirmitatem nostram*,[37] it will be referred to in the remainder of this Preface as the "new" *cantus firmus*.

Stylistically, this three-part work (i.e., no. [24]) belongs to the late fifteenth century, and it seems roughly contemporary with no. [2]. Because of its probable primacy, and because it may well be the original source of the "new" *cantus firmus* (although derivation from an as yet unidentified source cannot be ruled out), no. [24] is placed here at the head of the settings of this "new" *cantus firmus*. The principal source for no. [24] is London, British Library, Add. MS 35087, an early sixteenth-century *chansonnier* probably of Flemish origin, since it contains many Flemish songs. This work is only partially texted in the London source; the full refrain text appears in the source *Chansons a troys*. A medial cadence is easily made in m. 30, and a normal *rondeau* is apparently intended (to the full text used in nos. [1a] and [1b]). However, the tenor does not contain sufficient notes for all five lines of text; therefore line 2 is omitted in this edition, despite the presence of an incipit in the London manuscript. Moreover, the concordant *Chansons a troys* is of no aid in resolving this problem, as its tenor is lost.

Note to the Transcription

(1) The London MS (the source) gives the following incipit in all voices: "Fors seulement latente que je meure Et mon las cuer." The full text for S. and Ct. is found in *Chansons a troys* (Venice, 1520), which lacks the T.

[25] [Anonymous]

Sources
*Bologna, Civico Museo Bibliografico Musicale, MS Q 19, fols. 3'-4 (S., A., T., B.).

St. Gall, Stiftsbibliothek, MS 463, no. 193, "Fors seulement . . . Primum," "Dorius.i.Primus" (S., A., 5ta).

St. Gall, Stiftsbibliothek, MS 464, fol. 9 (S., B.).

Hewitt list: No. 28.

Commentary

The Bologna manuscript (dated 1518) contains the four-voice composition that constitutes the original form of this work. St. Gall 463 includes a fifth voice (labeled Vagans. Quinta Vox) that clearly was added to a self-contained entity—this added voice sometimes contradicts the harmony (see mm. 15, 18, 31, 32, 35, 42, 43, 46, 50) of the four-voice version. This fifth voice is included in this edition for the sake of completeness; however, it can and should be omitted in performance, if a proper hearing of the original work is desired.

The tenor of no. [24]—the "new" *cantus firmus*—serves here as superius (omitting m. 49), while the first eight measures of the altus in no. [25] state Ockeghem's superius, condensing the first two measures into one. A rapid, apparently instrumental figure in the lower voices may have been derived from Ockeghem's contratenor. Despite the clear reference to Ockeghem's work, this setting is based primarily on the "new" *cantus firmus*, which stands out in relief in the superius. Whether this melody is derived from no. [24] or from a common source cannot be determined with certainty.

Although the St. Gall manuscripts give the lengthy incipit "Fors seulement l'attente que je meure" in the superius, the markedly instrumental motives in the other voices make it unlikely that vocal performance is intended. Like no. [13], this piece was copied into MS 463 by the Swiss scholar Aegidius Tschudi, who numbered the two compositions "Primum" and "Secundum," and applied modal designations according to the system of his teacher, Heinrich Glareanus.[38] Tschudi probably derived the unfortunate *quinta vox* from MS 464, which he owned, since the surviving parts of the latter source are headed "a 5."

Notes to the Transcription

(1) M. 46, *quinta vox*, notes 3-6, this passage is so awkward that it should be omitted. For a substitute, the editor suggests a Sb. (half-note) on a.

(2) M. 47, S., an extra Sb. (a) appears in this m. in the source.

[26] [Matthaeus Pipelare]

Sources and Editions

Basel, Universitäts-Bibliothek, MSS F.X.1-4, no. 118, "Mathias Pipilari."

Bologna, Civico Museo Bibliografico Musicale, MS Q 19, fols. 1'-2, "Piplare."

Brussels, Bibliothèque royale, MS 228, fols. 17'-18, anon.

Brussels, Bibliothèque royale, MS IV.90 (S.), fols. 22'-23; Tournai, Bibliothèque de Ville, MS 94 (T.), fols. 22-22', anon.

*Florence, Biblioteca Nazionale Centrale, MS Magl. XIX.164-167, no. LXI, anon.

Paris, Bibliothèque nationale, fonds français MS 1597, fols. lx'-lxi, anon.

Regensburg, Proske-Bibliothek, MS C.120 (Pernner Codex), pp. 336-337, "Pipelare."

St. Gall, Stiftsbibliothek, MS 461, pp. 8-9, "M. Pipelare."

Segovia, Catedral, Archivo Musical, MS (without signature), p. xcii, "Matheus Pipe(lare)" (text: "Exortum est in tenebris").

Canti B (Venice: O. Petrucci, 1502), fols. 31'-32, "Pe. de la Rue."

In dissem Buechlyn fynt man LXXV. hubscher Lieder (Cologne: Arnt von Aich, ca. 1519), no. 72, anon.

[*Lieder*, Frankfurt: C. Egenolff, ca. 1535], I, no. XXXI, anon. (S. in Paris, Bibliothèque nationale, Rés. Vm7 504.)

Modern editions:

M. Pipelare, *Opera omnia*, ed. R. Cross (American Institute of Musicology, 1966-67), I: 11, 14, 34; E. Bernoulli and H. J. Moser, eds., *Das Liederbuch des Arnt von Aich* (Kassel, 1930), p. 126; E. Bernoulli, *Aus Liederbüchern der Humanistenzeit* (Leipzig, 1910), Beilage, no. XII; also Giesbert, *Ein altes Spielbuch*, p. 8 (after St. Gall 461); H. Hewitt, ed., *Canti B. numero cinquanta* (Chicago, 1967), p. 168; R.-J. van Maldeghem, ed., *Trésor musicale, Musique profane*, I (Brussels, 1865): no. 6 (with new text); XXI (1885): no. 12; J. Obrecht, *Werken*, ed. J. Wolf (Amsterdam, s.d.), VII: *Wereldlijke Werken*, p. 88 (after Florence 164-167); M. Picker, ed., *The Chanson Albums of Marguerite of Austria* (Berkeley, 1965), p. 233 (after Brussels 228); A. Seay, ed., *Pierre Attaingnant: Transcriptions of Chansons for Keyboard* (1531) (American Institute of Musicology, 1961), no. 10.

Hewitt list: No. 30.

Commentary

The tenor of no. [24]—the "new" *cantus firmus*—serves as tenor for this piece, with its introductory rests expanded here from eight to twelve measures. Many reflections of the melodic, harmonic, textural, and structural features of no. [24] exist in Pipelare's enormously popular setting; but it contains no reference to Ockeghem's "Fors seulement."[39]

Although it has a few misreadings of the French text, the Florence manuscript (the primary source for this edition) offers the most careful text underlay among the sources, despite its Italian (probably Florentine) origin. The placement of the third line of text remains problematic, however, and the medial cadence is difficult to locate. Because of this uncertainty, the remaining stanzas of the *rondeau* probably are not intended to be sung.

Notes to the Transcription

(1) In the source, the opening words of the text are given as "Forseullement."

(2) Mm. 26 ff., the source has "my lespoir" in all voices, an evident misreading.

(3) Mm. 44 ff., T., the source gives the text "pour ce doleur. . . ." This is a scribal error.

[27] [Anonymous]

Source and Edition

*Cambrai, Bibliothèque de Ville, MS 124, fol. 144'.

Modern edition: R.-J. van Maldeghem, ed., *Trésor musicale, Musique profane* (Brussels, 1882), XVIII: 8 (with substitute text).

Hewitt list: No. 33.

Commentary

The tenor of no. [24], transposed down an octave, is the basis of the tenor of this composition. However, additional rests are interpolated into the "new" *cantus firmus*, a few rhythmic changes are made (notably in m. 41), and a new phrase is inserted (mm. 46-49). The superius of this piece anticipates the melody of the tenor at the beginning of the setting and occasionally thereafter (see mm. 36 and 55). No reference is made to Ockeghem's setting, but Hewitt sees a reference to Févin's "Fors seulement" setting (no. [28]) in the altus of no. [27] at m. 25;[40] this reference occurs so casually, however, that it may well be a coincidence. There is no hint of a text beyond the incipit for this piece in the source. The active, disjunct melodies are not easily fitted with text, and instrumental performance is suggested.

NOTE TO THE TRANSCRIPTION

(1) M. 31, A., note 3 is f' in the source, making parallel fifths with the S.

[28] Anth[oine] de Févin

SOURCES AND EDITIONS

*Cambridge, University Library, Pepys MS 1760, fols. lviii'-lx, "Anth. de fevin."

Copenhagen, Kongelige Bibliotek, Ny Kgl. Saml. MS 1848-2°, pp. 102-103, anon.

London, British Library, Add. MS 31922, fols. 104'-105, anon.

Munich, Bayerische Staatsbibliothek, Mus. MS 1516, no. 129, anon. (transposed down a fifth).

Paderborn, Erzbischöfliche Akademische Bibliothek, Fürstenbergiana MS 9822/23, fol. 23 (S.), fol. 24 (Ct.), anon. (T. lacking).

St. Gall, Stiftsbibliothek, MS 463, no. 46, anon. (S. only).

Chansons a troys (Venice: A. Antico & L. A. Giunta, 1520), fols. 4-4' (S.), 52'-53 (Ct.), anon. (T. lacking).

[*Lieder*, Frankfurt: C. Egenolff, ca. 1535], III, no. LI, anon. (S. in Paris, Bibliothèque nationale, Rés. Vm7 504).

Trium vocum carmina (Nuremberg: H. Formschneider, 1538), no. 31, anon. (transposed down a fifth).

Trium vocum cantiones (Nuremberg: J. Petreius, 1541), no. 73, anon. ("Josquin" written in Jena copy).

Tiers livre de chansons (Paris: A. Le Roy & R. Ballard, 1553), no. 11, "Févin."

Premier livre de chansons (Paris: A. Le Roy & R. Ballard, 1578), fols. 12'-13, "Févin."

Modern editions:
Music at the Court of Henry VIII, ed. J. Stevens, Musica Britannica, XVIII (London, 1962), p. 76 (after London MS 31922); J. Obrecht, *Werken*, ed. J. Wolf, VII: *Wereldlijke Werken*, p. 90 (after *Trium vocum cantiones*); E. Geneti (Carpentras), *Opera omnia*, ed. A. Seay (American Institute of Musicology, 1972-73), I: 150 (after *Tiers livre*).

Hewitt list: No. 31.

COMMENTARY

The present transcription of the music of this popular piece is based on an English manuscript of Henry VIII's reign, while the text is taken here from *Chansons a troys*, printed in Venice in 1520 (see Texts and Translations). The poem in the latter source is a well-wrought parody of the original refrain ("Fors seulement la mort, sans nul autre attente..."), and is also found in St. Gall 463 and in Le Roy & Ballard's editions. The Cambridge manuscript begins with the same first line in the superius, but continues thereafter with the familiar text ("que je meure, En mon las cuer..."). Other concordant sources have only the incipit "Fors seulement." Févin probably used the new text for his setting, since it is associated with his music in such widely dispersed sources. This new text may originally have been a full *rondeau*, since a medial cadence can be managed in m. 37. However, additional verses are lacking in all sources.

Musically, no. [28] is among the most interesting of all "Fors seulement" settings. It is a parody, primarily of no. [26] but also, to a lesser extent, of no. [24]. The reworking of motives of earlier compositions was still a novel technique at the beginning of the sixteenth century (Févin died in 1512), and this must be one of the earliest examples of a chanson composed in this manner. The opening motive, for example, is a free elaboration of the opening theme of no. [26]. Févin's motive may have been suggested, moreover, by m. 45 of the contra of no. [24]. Throughout no. [28], Févin draws upon both of his models (nos. [24] and [26]); however, because nos. [24] and [26] are so closely related, it is sometimes difficult to be certain which of the two is his principal source.

NOTES TO THE TRANSCRIPTION

(1) M. 2, T., note 4 is b' in the source.

(2) M. 56, S., the source has a superfluous e'' (Sm.) following note 4.

[29] Jörg Blanckenmüller

SOURCE

*Munich, Bayerische Staatsbibliothek, Mus. MS 1516, no. 131, "Jörg blanckenmüller."

Hewitt list: No. 32.

COMMENTARY

At its beginning, this setting only vaguely suggests the motives of nos. [24]-[28]; but from m. 40 on, this work asserts itself as a parody of no. [28], taking its point of departure from mm. 49-54 of Févin's setting. Nothing is known of Blanckenmüller, but he is believed to have been active in southern Germany around 1540.[41] Except for an incipit, the source carries no text, and, therefore, instrumental performance is appropriate, especially in view of the irregular phrase-lengths and the constant rhythmic activity of the parts.

[30] Adrianus Willa[e]rt

SOURCES AND EDITIONS

Copenhagen, Kongelige Bibliotek, Gl. Kgl. Saml., MS 1873-4°, (T.,) fol. 32, anon. (A. missing).

Selectissimae necnon familiarissimae cantiones (Augsburg, M. Kriesstein, 1540), no. XLIII, "Adrianus Willart."

Hewitt list: No. 35.

COMMENTARY

This setting, like de Sylva's (no. [11]), is for low voices ("ad equales voces"). The tenor of Févin's setting (no. [28]), transposed down a fifth, serves as the superius of Willaert's setting, while Willaert's 5ta quotes the first four measures of Févin's contra in a similar transposition. The text is that of no. [28], although there are a few slight variants.

It is noteworthy that no. [30], one of the latest members of the "Fors seulement" family, is a traditional *cantus firmus* setting, even though its specific model is a parody. No better illustration of Willaert's essential conservatism can be found, nor can the co-existence of traditional and innovative techniques in sixteenth-century music be exemplified more strikingly.

Acknowledgments

Those who contributed materials and assistance of one kind or another for this edition are legion, and I can only hope to single out a few. Above all is Helen Hewitt, whose paper "*Fors seulement* and the Cantus Firmus Technique of the Fifteenth Century," read at the annual meeting of the American Musicological Society in Berkeley in December 1960 and subsequently published in *Essays in Musicology in Honor of Dragan Plamenac*, ed. by Gustave Reese and Robert J. Snow (Pittsburgh, 1969), pp. 91-126, created the framework for the present study. Dr. Hewitt and I corresponded frequently on various aspects of the subject, and shortly before her death she graciously ceded to me her plan to publish the entire corpus of *Fors seulement* compositions. I am also indebted to Professor Nino Pirrotta for his helpful suggestions, and to Professor Richard Wexler for assistance in locating sources. The Herzog-August-Bibliothek, Wolfenbüttel; the Library of Congress, Washington, D.C.; and the British Library, London, generously provided the photographs reproduced here. The many other libraries that supplied microfilms are listed among the sources for the thirty settings in this edition. Libraries and institutions that permitted me to consult their microfilm holdings include the following: the University of California, Berkeley; the Isham Library of Harvard University; the School of Music of the University of Illinois at Champaign-Urbana; Princeton University; and Rutgers University. Support for the research that led to this edition came from many institutions over a long period, principally Harvard University, which granted me an I Tatti Fellowship in 1966-1967; the National Endowment for the Humanities, which awarded me a Senior Fellowship in 1972-1973; and the Research Council of Rutgers University. I am also grateful to the staff of A-R Editions, Inc., for their careful editing and preparation of this edition for publication. Finally, I wish to thank my wife, Ruth, for her patience and forebearance while this work was accomplished.

Martin Picker
Rutgers University
New Brunswick, New Jersey

April 1981

Notes

1. All the secular works and motets are listed in Helen Hewitt, "*Fors seulement* and the Cantus Firmus Technique of the Fifteenth Century," in *Essays in Musicology in Honor of Dragan Plamenac*, ed. Gustave Reese and Robert J. Snow (Pittsburgh, 1969), pp. 91-126. Dr. Hewitt's work has been an essential foundation for the present edition.

One correction to the Hewitt list should be noted: No. 21 is actually the complete Benedictus of Obrecht's *Missa Fors seulement* and thus does not belong in the list.

Dr. Hewitt does not list the Masses. Five have been identified, and all are available in the following modern editions: (1) Johannes Ockeghem, *Collected Works*, ed. Dragan Plamenac (American Musicological Society, 1947-), II: 65; (2) Jacob Obrecht, *Werken*, ed. Johannes Wolf (Amsterdam, 1908-1921), *Missen*, V: 133; (3) Matthaeus Pipelare, *Opera omnia*, ed. Ronald Cross (American Institute of Musicology, 1966-67), II: 82; (4) Nicolas Gombert, *Opera omnia*, ed. Joseph Schmidt-Görg (American Institute of Musicology, 1951-), II: 89; (5) Elzéar Genet (Carpentras), *Opera omnia*, ed. Albert Seay (American Institute of Musicology, 1972-73), I: 91.

Ockeghem and Obrecht based their Masses on the original *rondeau*. Pipelare modeled his on other "Fors seulement" settings (see nos. [24] and [26] of this edition); Gombert used still other settings (see nos. [26] and [28]); and Carpentras used the setting transcribed here as no. [28].

2. For biographical information on these composers, see

Gustave Reese, *Music in the Renaissance*, rev. ed. (New York, 1959), chap. 5, *passim*, and *The New Grove Dictionary of Music and Musicians*, ed. Stanley Sadie (London, 1980).

3. It is possible that the famous Alexander Agricola (d. 1506) rather than the obscure Johannes, is actually the composer of the "Fors seulement" setting; see the Commentary on no. [9].

4. See Hewitt, *"Fors seulement,"* pp. 93 ff. For further information about these composers, see Reese, *Music in the Renaissance*, chaps. 5-7.

5. See Lewis Lockwood, "A View of the Early Sixteenth-Century Parody Mass," in *Department of Music, Queens College, Twenty-fifth Anniversary Festschrift* (New York, 1964), pp. 53-77; also idem, "On 'Parody' as Term and Concept in 16th-Century Music," in *Aspects of Medieval and Renaissance Music*, ed. Jan LaRue (New York, 1966), pp. 560-575.

6. There is a modern edition of this manuscript by F. J. Giesbert, *Ein altes Spielbuch: Liber Fridolini Sichery* (Mainz, 1936). Giesbert's edition is useful, but it is not scholarly, and it contains more than a few errors.

7. For a description and summary of recent research on the MS Basevi, see Martin Staehelin, "Quellenkundliche Beiträge zum Werk von Johannes Ghiselin-Verbonnet," *Archiv für Musikwissenschaft* XXIV (1967): 123-125.

8. For a recent description and summary of current research, see Jaap van Benthem, "Eine wiedererkannte Josquin-Chansons im Codex 18746 der Österreichischen Nationalbibliothek," *Tijdschrift van de Vereniging voor Nederlandse Muziekgeschiedenis* XXII-1 (1971): 18 ff.

9. See Franz Krautwurst, "Pernner-Kodex," in *Die Musik in Geschichte und Gegenwart* (Kassel, 1962), X: cols. 1075-1076.

10. August Wilhelm Ambros, *Geschichte der Musik*, 3rd ed. (Leipzig, 1887-1911), III: 57.

11. Otto Gombosi, *Jacob Obrecht: Ein stilkritische Studie* (Leipzig, 1925), pp. 16 ff.

12. See note 1, above.

13. These are: (1) Hewitt No. 11 (Bologna, Civico Museo Bibliografico Musicale, MS R. 142, fol. 57'), of which the lone surviving part, inscribed "Josquin a sei," is identical to Ockeghem's superius; and (2) Hewitt No. 12 (Cortona, Bibl. Com. MSS 95-96, fols. 20'-21; Paris, Bibl. nat. n.a.fr. 1817, fols. 23-23'), an anonymous 4-part setting in which Ockeghem's superius, transposed down an octave, serves as tenor, and of which the bassus part is missing. Hewitt No. 21 is erroneously described as "incomplete"; actually, it is the Benedictus of Obrecht's *Missa Fors seulement* (see note 1, above).

14. These are: (1) Hewitt No. 24, an anonymous 5-part "Maria mater gratie," based on Ockeghem's tenor, printed in Martin Picker, ed., *The Chanson Albums of Marguerite of Austria* (Berkeley, 1965), p. 257; and (2) Hewitt No. 34, Philippe Verdelot's "Infirmitatem nostram" for 5 voices, based on the "new" *cantus firmus* (see nos. [24]-[27] of the present edition), printed in A. Smijers, ed., *Treize livres de motets parus chez Pierre Attaingant en 1534 et 1535* (Paris, 1934-1964), IV: 99.

15. Hewitt, *"Fors seulement,"* p. 93. Festa's lost setting may be the composition discussed in a letter dated 1514 to Cardinal Ippolito I d'Este of Ferrara from an emissary in Rome: "I am herewith sending to your excellency a *Fors seulement* for three voices, which I am sure will please you, even if its composer is an Italian." See Lewis Lockwood, "Jean Mouton and Jean Michel," *Journal of the American Musicological Society* XXXII (1979): 217.

Also unrelated to Ockeghem's *rondeau* is Josquin Baston's "Fors seulement rigeur tormente" in Tilman Susato's *Le huictiesme livre des chansons a quatre parties* (Antwerp, 1545), fol. 10.

16. Concerning the shift in relative durations around 1450, see Willi Apel, *The Notation of Polyphonic Music 900-1600*, 4th ed. (Cambridge, Mass., 1953), p. 97, note 1.

17. The bibliography for these manuscripts is extensive. A fundamental study is Knud Jeppesen, ed., *Der Kopenhagener Chansonnier* (Copenhagen, 1927; new ed., New York, 1965), pp. xxiv ff. A facsimile edition of *Dijon, Bibliothèque publique, Manuscript 517*, with an introduction by Dragan Plamenac, is published by the Institute of Mediaeval Music (Brooklyn, s.d.). See also Helen E. Bush, "The Laborde *Chansonnier*," *Papers of the American Musicological Society 1940* (New York, 1946), pp. 56-79. For a facsimile of the pages of the Laborde manuscript containing no. [1a], see Plate III.

Jeppesen believes that the hand in which this piece is written is the earliest in the Laborde manuscript, but Bush, following Oliver Strunk, considers it second in chronology, despite its archaic appearance (sharply pointed note heads, long stems). The assertion that the manuscripts were written at the Burgundian court in Dijon is supported by no evidence other than the preservation of the principal *chansonnier* of this group in that city.

18. See the discussion by Jeppesen, *Der Kopenhagener Chansonnier*, pp. xxiv ff. Jeppesen does not assign a date, but describes the manuscript as being in a later fifteenth-century hand, postdating most of Dijon and the part of Laborde containing Ockeghem's chanson.

19. See Jeanne Marix, "Hayne van Ghizeghem," *The Musical Quarterly* XXVIII (1942): 282.

20. Gombosi, *Jacob Obrecht*, pp. 18 ff.

21. This manuscript is one of a large group associated with the Hapsburg-Burgundian court at Mechelen and Brussels between ca. 1490 and 1530. See Herbert Kellman, "The Origins of the Chigi Codex," *Journal of the American Musicological Society* XI (1958): 6-19, and idem, "Josquin and the Courts of the Netherlands and France," *Josquin des Prez, Proceedings of the International Josquin Festival-Conference . . . 1971*, ed. Edward E. Lowinsky (London, 1976), pp. 195 and 209. See also Martin Staehelin, "Quellenkundliche Beiträge," cited in note 7 above.

22. The case for musical symbolism referring to this text is presented in Picker, *The Chanson Albums of Marguerite of Austria*, p. 68.

23. See the article "Reyngoot" in René Vannes, *Dictionnaire des Musiciens* (Brussels, 1947), pp. 342 ff.

24. Concerning de Orto's special interest in *musica ficta*, see Picker, *The Chanson Albums of Marguerite of Austria*, p. 96.

25. An untexted work for 3 voices is attributed to "Jannes Agricola" in Florence, Bibl. Naz. Centr. MS Banco Rari 229, fols. 21'-22; see Bianca Becherini, *Catalogo dei Manoscritti Musicali della Biblioteca Nazionale di Firenze* (Kassel, 1959), p. 23.

26. For a searching, if somewhat speculative, consideration of the origin of Bologna MS Q 19, see Edward E. Lowinsky, *The Medici Codex of 1518 . . . Historical Introduction and Commentary* (Chicago, 1968), pp. 52 ff.

27. See Lowinsky, *The Medici Codex*, pp. 141 ff., 205-213; also Winfried Kirsch, *Die Motetten des Andreas de Silva* (Tutzing, 1977), pp. 11 ff., and the review of the same by David Crawford in *Journal of the American Musicological Society* XXXII (1979): 150-155. See also *The New Grove Dictionary of Music and Musicians*, s.v. "De Silva," by Winfried Kirsch.

28. See Jaap van Benthem, "Einige wiedererkannte Josquin-Chansons," pp. 18 ff.

29. See Kellman, "Origins of the Chigi Codex" and "Josquin and the Courts of the Netherlands and France." The Vienna and Brussels manuscripts are compared in Martin Picker, "The Chanson Albums of Marguerite of Austria," *Annales Musicologiques* VI (1958-1963): 155-157.

30. See Donald G. Loach, "Aegidius Tschudi's Songbook (St. Gall MS 463): A Humanistic Document from the Circle of Heinrich Glarean," 2 vols. (Ph.D. diss., University of California, Berkeley, 1969; University Microfilms UM 70-17,607).

31. See *The New Grove Dictionary of Music and Musicians*, s.v. "Divitis," by Martin Picker. Concerning Bologna MS Q 19, see Lowinsky, *The Medici Codex*.

32. Gombosi, *Jacob Obrecht*, p. 25.

33. Clytus Gottwald, *Johannes Ghiselin—Johannes Verbonnet* (Wiesbaden, 1962), p. 103.

34. Helmuth Osthoff, *Josquin Desprez* (Tutzing, 1964-1965), II: 301.

35. This was first pointed out in Martin Staehelin, "Möglichkeiten und praktische Anwendung der Verfasserbestimmung an anonym überlieferten Kompositionen der Josquin-Zeit," *Tijdschrift van de Vereniging voor Nederlandse Muziekgeschiedenis* XXIII-2 (1973): 81 ff. The same conclusion was reached independently by Joshua Rifkin in a paper, "Josquin and Agricola in an Augsburg Source," read at the Symposium on the French Chanson held in honor of Gustave Reese at New York University on 1 July 1974. The manuscript is described in Martin Bente, *Neue Weg der Quellenkritik und die Biographie Ludwig Senfls* (Wiesbaden, 1968), p. 234.

36. See Jaap van Benthem, "Einige wiedererkannte," and the commentary to no. [12].

37. See note 14.

38. See Loach, "Aegidius Tschudi's Songbook," and the commentary to no. [13].

39. Concerning the indebtedness of Pipelare's setting to no. [24], see Picker, *The Chanson Albums of Marguerite of Austria*, pp. 74 ff. Compare, also, Pipelare's first setting, no. [5] above.

40. Hewitt, "*Fors seulement*," p. 117.

41. See the articles by Hans-Christian Müller in *Die Musik in Geschichte und Gegenwart*, XV: 830-831, and *The New Grove Dictionary of Music and Musicians*, II: 778-779.

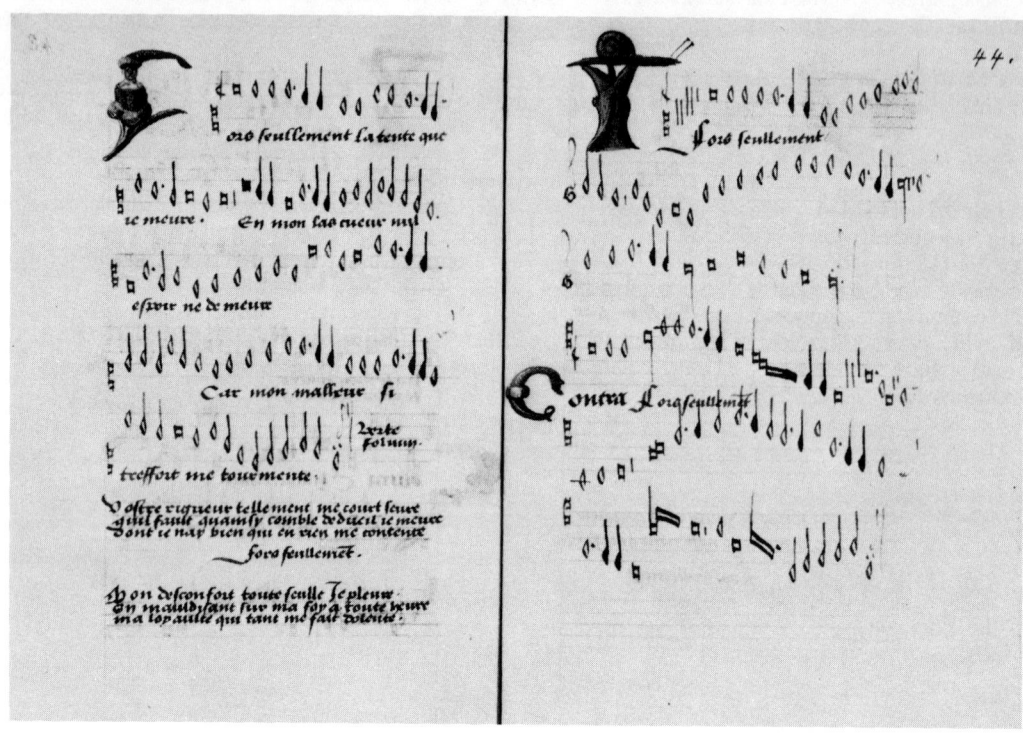

Plate I. Wolfenbüttel, Herzog-August-Bibliothek, MS 287 Extravag., fols. 43'-44.
(Ockeghem, no. [1b], first part)

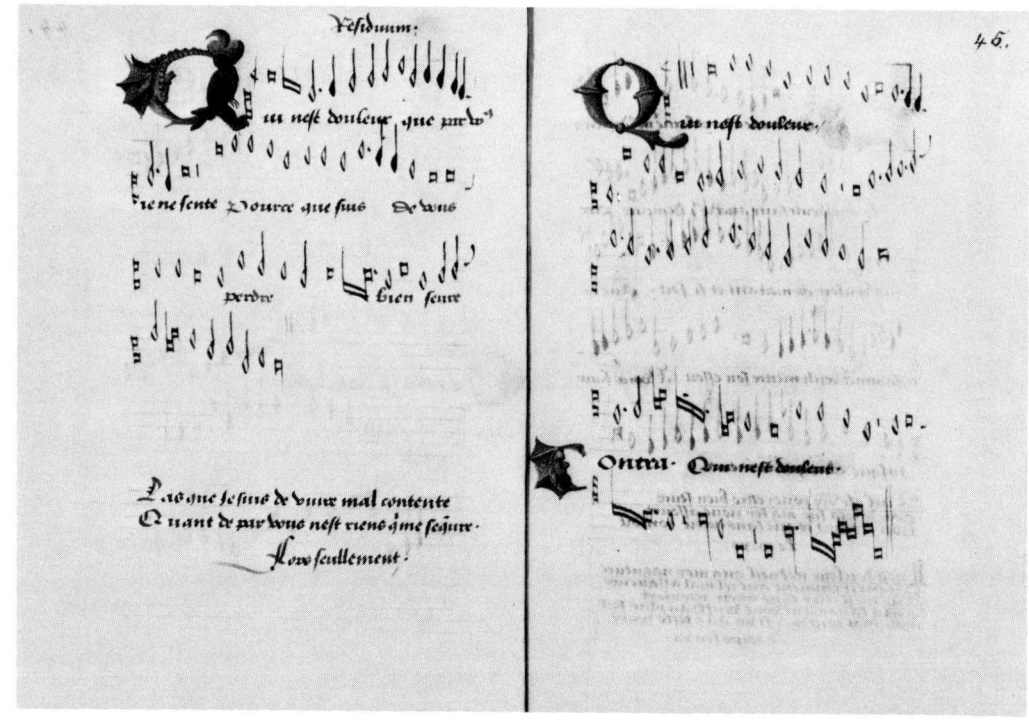

Plate II. Wolfenbüttel, Herzog-August-Bibliothek, MS 287 Extravag., fols. 44'-45.
(Ockeghem, no. [1b], second part)

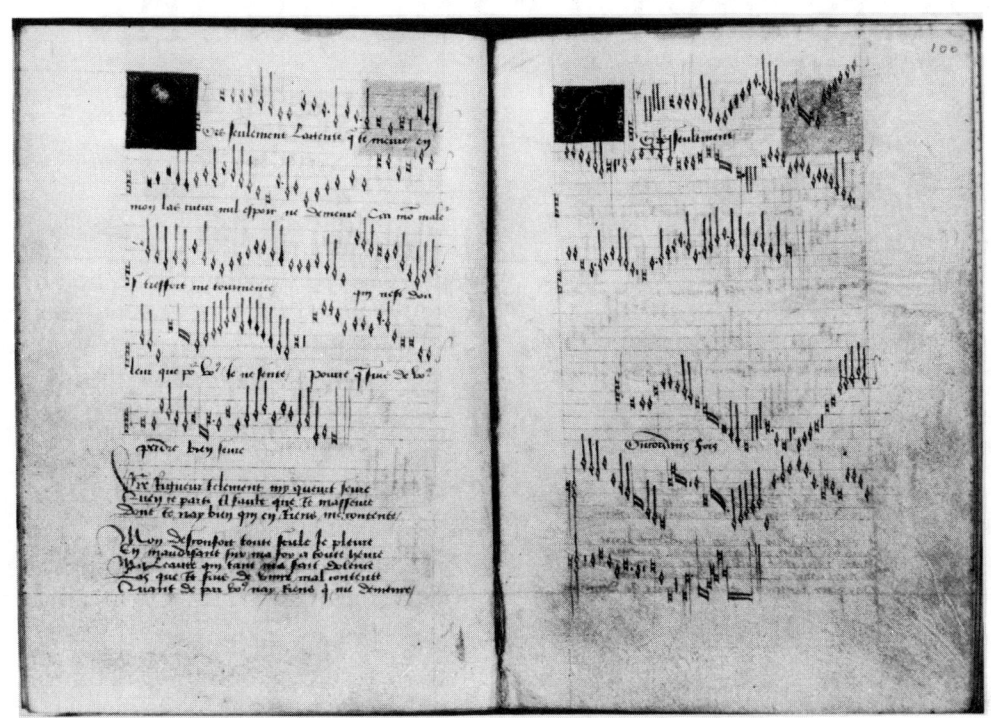

Plate III. Washington, D.C., Library of Congress, M2.1 L25 Case (MS Laborde), fols. 99'-100. (Ockeghem, concordant source for no. [1a])

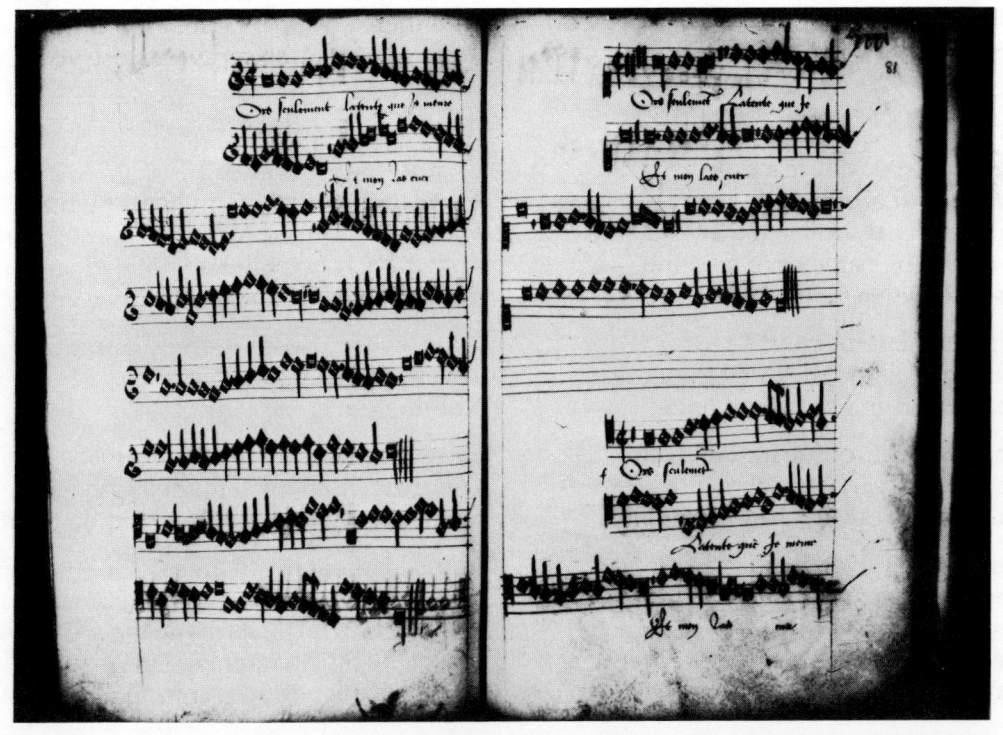

Plate IV. London, British Library, Add. MS 35087, fols. 80'-81. (Anon., no. [24])

Texts and Translations*

[1a] *(after Dijon MS 517 and Washington MS Laborde)*

Fors seulement l'actente que je meure,
En mon las cueur nul espoir ne demeure,
Car mon maleur si tresfort me tourmente
Qu'il n'est douleur que pour vous je ne sente
Pource que suis de vous perdre bien seure.

Vostre rigeur tellement m'y queurt seure,
Qu' en ce parti il fault que je m'asseure
Dont je n'ay bien qui en riens me contente.

Fors seulement l'actente que je meure,
En mon las cueur nul espoir ne demeure,
Car mon maleur si tresfort me tourmente.

Mon desconfort toute seule je pleure,
En maudisant, sur ma foy, a toute heure,
Ma leauté qui tant m'a fait dolente.
Las, que je suis de vivre mal contente,
Quant de par vous n'ay riens qui me demeure.

Fors seulement l'actente que je meure,
En mon las cueur nul espoir ne demeure,
Car mon maleur si tresfort me tourmente
Qu'il n'est douleur que pour vous je ne sente
Pource que suis de vous perdre bien seure.

Except waiting for death,
There dwells in my faint heart no hope,
For my misfortune torments me so greatly
That there is no pain I do not feel on your account
Because I am quite certain to lose you.

Your severity does so surely pursue me,
That I must assure myself in this state
Nothing can content me.

Except waiting for death,
There dwells in my faint heart no hope,
For my misfortune torments me so greatly.

Alone I lament my distress,
In cursing, on my honor, at all times,
My loyalty which has made me so sorrowful.
Alas, I am little content to live,
Since I am left with nothing from you.

Except waiting for death,
There dwells in my faint heart no hope,
For my misfortune torments me so greatly
That there is no pain I do not feel on your account
Because I am quite certain to lose you.

[1b] *(after Wolfenbüttel MS 287)*

Fors seullement l'atente que je meure,
En mon las cueur nul espoir ne demeure,
Car mon malheur si tresfort me tourmente
Qui n'est douleur que par vous je ne sente,
Pource que suis de vous perdre bien seure.

Vostre rigeur tellement me court seure,
Qu'il fault qu'ainsy comblé de dueil je meure,
Dont je n'ay bien qui en rien me contente.

Fors seullement l'atente que je meure,
En mon las cueur nul espoir ne demeure,
Car mon malheur si tresfort me tourmente.

Mon desconfort toute seulle je pleure,
En mauldisant, sur ma foy, a toute heure,
Ma loyaulté qui tant me fait dolente.
Las, que je suis de vivre mal contente,
Quant de par vous n'est riens qui me sequeure.

Except waiting for death,
There dwells in my faint heart no hope,
For my misfortune torments me so greatly
That there is no pain I do not feel on your account,
Because I am quite certain to lose you.

Your severity does so surely pursue me,
That filled with grief I must die;
Nothing can content me.

Except waiting for death,
There dwells in my faint heart no hope,
For my misfortune torments me so greatly.

Alone I lament my distress,
In cursing, on my honor, at all times,
My loyalty which has made me so sorrowful.
Alas, I am little content to live,
Since there is no succour from you.

* See Texts and Performance Media for other pieces with these texts.

Fors seullement l'atente que je meure,
En mon las cueur nul espoir ne demeure,
Car mon malheur si tresfort me tourmente
Qui n'est douleur que par vous je ne sente,
Pource que suis de vous perdre bien seure.

Except waiting for death,
There dwells in my faint heart no hope,
For my misfortune torments me so greatly
That there is no pain I do not feel on your account,
Because I am quite certain to lose you.

[2] (after Paris MS 2245)

Fors seullement contre ce qu'ay promys,
Et en tous lieux seray fort entremis,
Et acquerray une belle aliance.
J'en ay desir voir des mon enfance,
Point ne vouldroye avoir nulz enemys.

Except for what I have promised,
I will be deeply involved everywhere,
And I will make a beautiful alliance.
Since my childhood I have wished it,
And I want no enemies.

Mon vouloir j'ay tout en cela soubmis,
Et hors dela ja ne serai transmis,
Garder ny veul ordre sens ne prudence.

I have entirely submitted my will,
And I will not now be moved from that,
Nor do I wish to preserve order, sense, and prudence.

Fors seullement contre ce qu'ay promis,
Et en tous lieux seray fort entremis,
Et acquiray une belle aliance.

Except for what I have promised,
I will be deeply involved everywhere,
And I will make a beautiful alliance.

Je cuide avoir en terre des amys,
Et que en eulx ay ma fiance mys.
On doibt sçavoir que n'ay nulle doubtance,
[Ou aultrement querroye ma deffiance]
Car je sçeray de tout honneur remis.

I imagine myself to have some friends in the land,
And I have put my trust in them.
One ought to know that I have no doubt.
[Otherwise I would pursue my defiance]
Because I would be denied all honor.

Fors seullement contre ce qu'ay promys,
Et en tous lieux seray fort entremis,
Et acqueray une belle aliance.
J'en ay desir voir des mon enfance,
Point ne vouldroye avoir nulz enemys.

Except for what I have promised,
I will be deeply involved everywhere,
And I will make a beautiful alliance.
Since my childhood I have wished it,
And I want no enemies.

[6] (after Brussels MS 228)

Du tout plongiet au lac de desespoir,
Trouvé me suis sans attente n'espoir
D'avoir jamais des biens de fortune;
Mais se trouver puis sçayson oportune,
Je me assairay d'en quelque chose avoir.

Plunged into the lake of despair by all,
I find myself without expectation or hope
Of ever having good fortune;
But if I can find the opportune time,
I will try to have something from it.

Regard el n'a, n'a vertu, n'a sçavoir;
Autant luy est mon valloir que valloir.
Parquoy demeure et sans resource aulcune.

She has no regard either for virtue or for knowledge;
It is the same to her to have or not have value.
Therefore I remain without any resource.

Du tout plongiet au lac de desespoir,
Trouvé me suis sans attente n'espoir
D'avoir jamais des biens de fortune;

Plunged into the lake of despair by all,
I find myself without expectation or hope
Of ever having good fortune;

Se j'eusse sçeu le temps future prevoir,
Et a mon cas de piecha pourveoir
A amasser quelque peu de pecune,
Pour le present ne fusse en moy fortune
La ou je suis sy me fault ramanoir.

If I had known how to foresee the future,
And long ago to provide for my situation
By amassing a little money,
For the present it would not have been my fortune
That I must remain where I am.

Du tout plongiet au lac de desespoir,
Trouvé me suis sans attente n'espoir
D'avoir jamais des biens de fortune;
Mais se trouver puis sçayson oportune,
Je me assairay d'en quelque chose avoir.

Plunged into the lake of despair by all,
I find myself without expectation or hope
Of ever having good fortune;
But if I can find the opportune time,
I will try to have something from it.

[28] *(after Chansons a troys, 1520)*

Fors seullement la mort, sans nul autre attente,
De reconfort, souz douloureuse tante,
Ay pris se jour despiteuse demeure,
Comme celuy qui desolé demeure
Prochain d'ennuy et loing de son attente.

Without any other expectation, except death,
Of comfort, under so much sorrow,
I have today taken a position of scorn,
As one who, desolate, remains
Near to woe and far from his goal.

THIRTY SETTINGS OF "FORS SEULEMENT"

[1a]

[Johannes] O[c]keghem

[1b]

[Johannes Ockeghem]

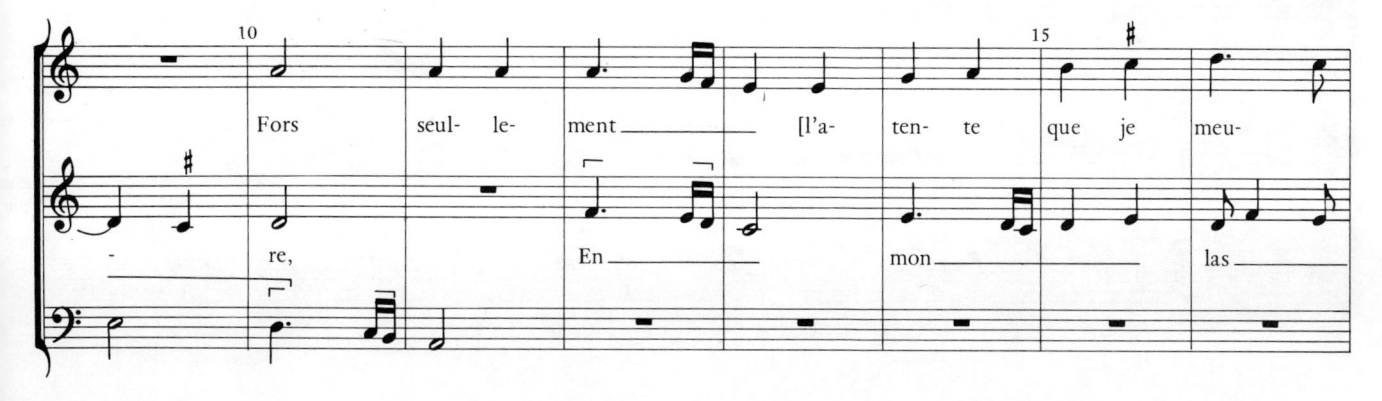

Fors seullement

de- meu- re, Car mon mal- heur si tres- fort me tour- men- te]
ne de- meu- - - re, Car mon mal- heur si tres- fort me tour- - - men- - te
Qui n'est dou- leur [que par vous je ne sen- te,
Qui n'est dou- - leur
que par vous je ne sen- -

[2]

[Johannes] O[c]keghem

Canon / Royal
[Superius]
Tenor
Contra

Pour- ce que suis de- vous per- dre
-te, Pour- ce que suis de vous per-
- - dre bien seu- - re.]
- -dre bien seu- - - re.

Fors seul- - le- - ment con- tre
Fors seul- - le- ment
Fors seul- le- ment l'at- ten- te que je

ce qu'ay pro- mys, Et en tous lieux
[con- tre ce qu'ay pro- mys,] Et en tous
meu- - re, En mon las cueur nul e-

15
se- - ray fort
lieux, [et en tous lieux] se- ray
- spoir ne de- meu- re,
20
25
en- - - tre- mis,
fort en- tre- -
Car mon mal- heur [si tres- fort
30
Et ac- quer- ray u- - ne bel- - le a- li-
-mis, Et ac- quer- - ray u- ne bel- - le a-
me tour- men- te]
35
-an- - - - - ce. J'en
- li- an- - - - - ce. J'en ay
Qu'il n'est dou-

ay de- sir voir des mon en- fan- ce, [mon en-
de- - sir voir des mon en- fan- ce,
-leur que par vous [je ne sen- te]
-fan- ce,] Point ne voul- - -
[mon en- fan- ce,] Point ne voul- droy-
Pour- ce que suis de vous
-droy- e a- - voir nulz
-e a- - - voir nulz, [nulz]
per- - dre bien
e- - - - - ne- mis.
e- - - - ne- mis.
seu- - - re.

[3]

[Jacob] Hobrecht

e- - spoir
las cueur nul e- spoir ne de-
las cueur nul e- spoir ne
cueur nul e- spoir ne de-
ne de- - meu- - re, Car
-meu- re, Car mon mal- heur
de- - meu- re, Car mon mal- heur
-meu- re, Car mon mal- heur
mon mal- - heur si tres- fort me tour-
si- tres- fort me tour- men-
si tres- fort me tour- men- - -
si tres- fort me

40
- men- - te
-te
- - te Qu'il
tour- men- - - te
45
dou- - -
Qu'il n'est dou- leur que
n'est dou- leur que par vous je ne sen-
Qu'il n'est dou- leur que par vous je ne
50
-leur que par vous je ne sen- te
55
par vous je ne sen- te Pour-
-te Pour- - ce que suis de vous,
sen- te Pour- - ce

Pour- -ce que suis de vous per-
-ce que suis de vous
de
que de vous

-dre bien seu-
per- -dre bien
vous per- dre bien
per- -dre bien seu-

-re.]
seu- -re.]
seu- -re.]
-re.]

[4]

[Pierre de la] Rue

[Superius] Fors seullement

Contra Fors seullement

Tenor Fors seullement

Bassus Fors seullement

13

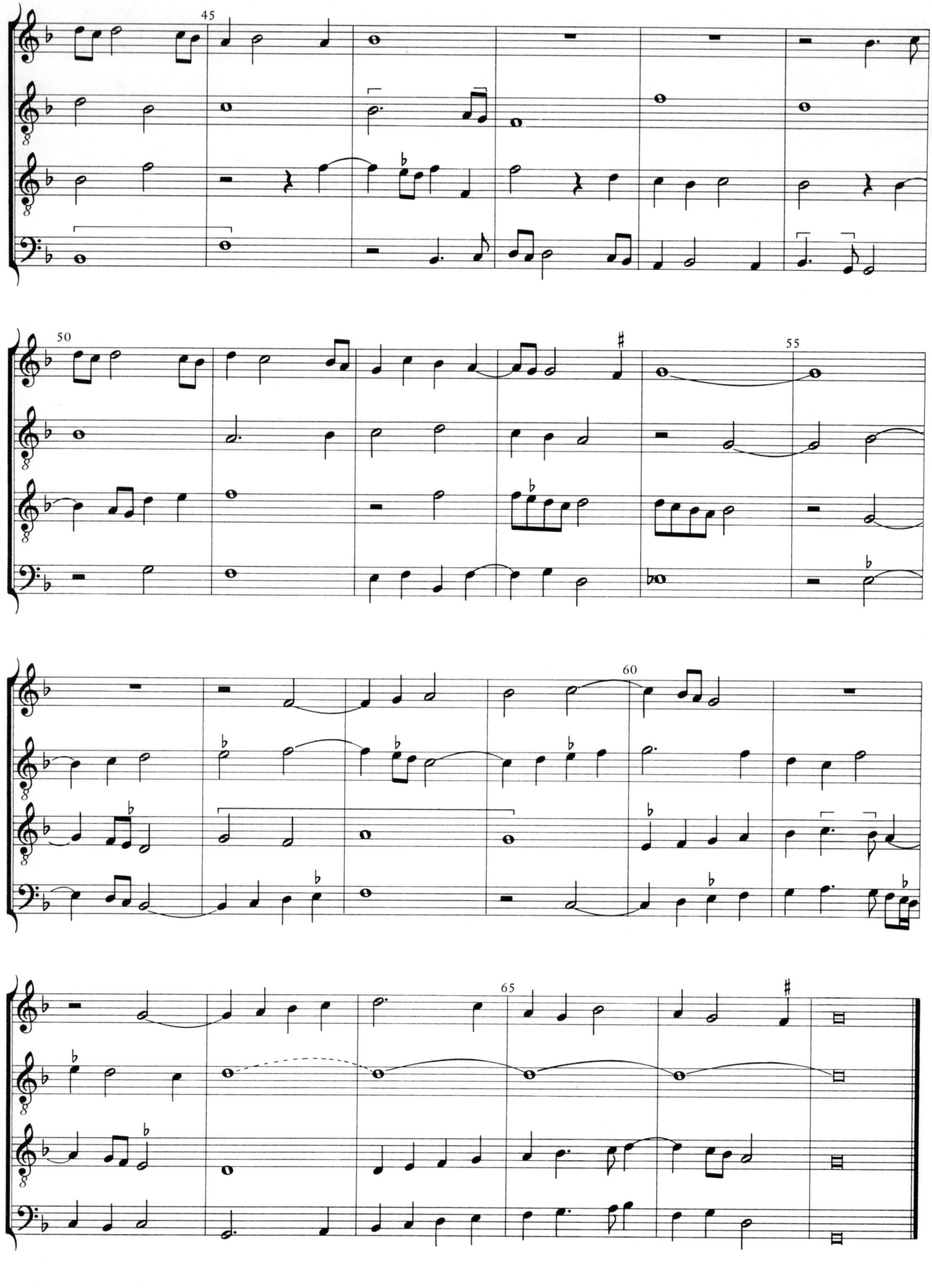
45
50
55
60
65

[5]

[Matthaeus] Pipelare

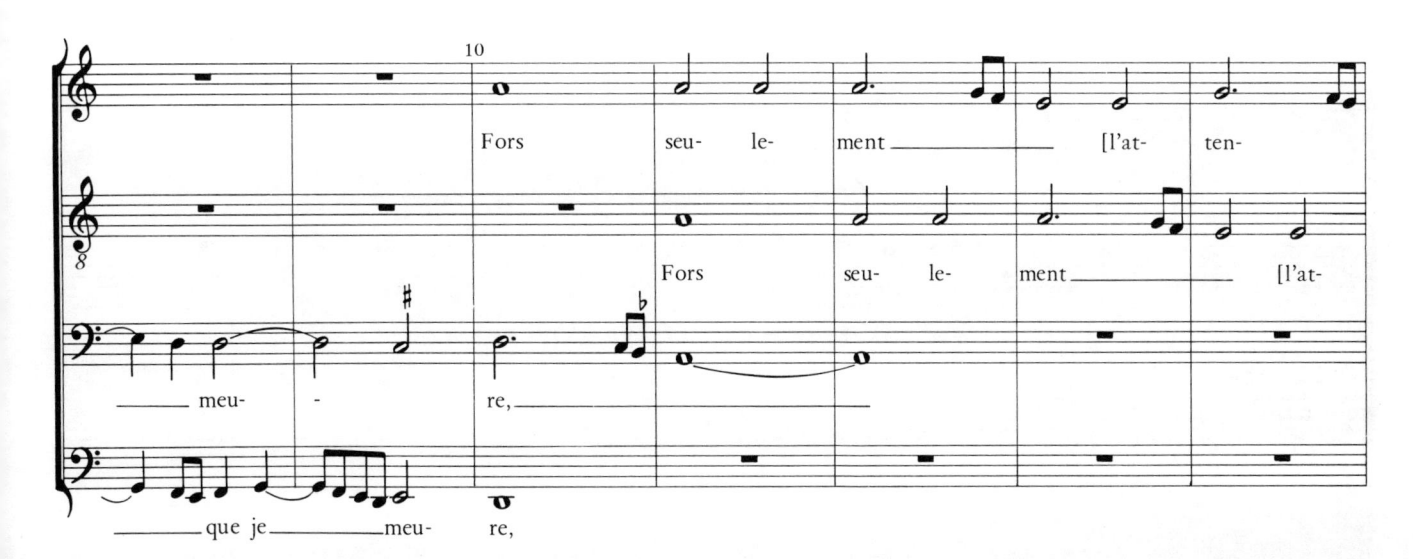

25
En mon las
las cueur nul e- spoir ne de- meu- re,
las cueur nul e- spoir ne de- - meu-
En mon las cueur nul e- -
30
35
cueur nul e- spoir ne de- meu- - re, Car
Car mon mal- heur si tres-
- - - re, Car
- spoir ne de-meu- re,
40
mon mal- heur tres- - fort me
-fort me tour- men- te]
mon mal- heur tres- - fort
Car mon mal-

tour- men- te Qu'il n'est dou-
Qu'il
me tour- men- te Qu'il n'est dou- leur que par
-heur tres fort me tour- men- te

-leur que par vous je ne sen- te Pour-
n'est dou- leur [que par vous je ne sen- te
vous je ne sen- te Pour-ce
Pour-

-ce que suis de
Pour- ce que suis de vous
que suis de
ce que suis de

[6]

[Antoine Brumel]

Du tout plongiet, [du tout plongiet
Fors seulement l'actente que
Du tout plongiet, [du tout plongiet] au
Du tout plongiet, [du tout plongiet, du tout plongiet]

-giet] au lac de des- - e-
je meu- re, [En mon las
lac de des- - e- spoir, Trou-
au lac de des- - e- spoir,
-spoir, Trou- - vé me suis sans at- - ten- te n'e- -
cueur nul e- spoir ne de- - meu-
- vé me suis sans at- ten- te
Trou-vé me suis sans at- ten- - te n'e- -
-spoir, [n'e- - - - spoir] D'a-
-re, Car mon mal- heur
n'e- spoir, [n'e- - - spoir]
-spoir, [n'e- - - spoir] D'a- -

20

-voir jamais des biens de for-
si tres- fort me tour- men-
D'a- voir jamais des biens
-voir jamais des biens

-tu- ne; Mais se trou- ver puis
-te de for- tu- ne;
de- for- tu- ne; Mais se trou-

Qu'il n'est dou-
Mais se trou- ver
-ver puis sçay- son o- por- tu-

40
45
sçay- son o- por- tu- - -
-leur que par vous je ne sen- te
puis sçay- son o- por- - tu- ne
-ne, [o- - por- tu- ne,] Je me as-
50
-ne, Je me as- - sai- -
Pour- ce que suis de vous
Je me as- sai- ray
-sai- - - ray
55
-ray, [je me as- - sai- - ray] d'en quel- que
per- - dre bien
d'en quel- que cho- - - -
d'en quel- - que cho-

cho- — — se a- — — voir.

seu- — — re.]

se a- — — — voir.

-se a- — — — — voir.

[7]

G[illes] Reingot

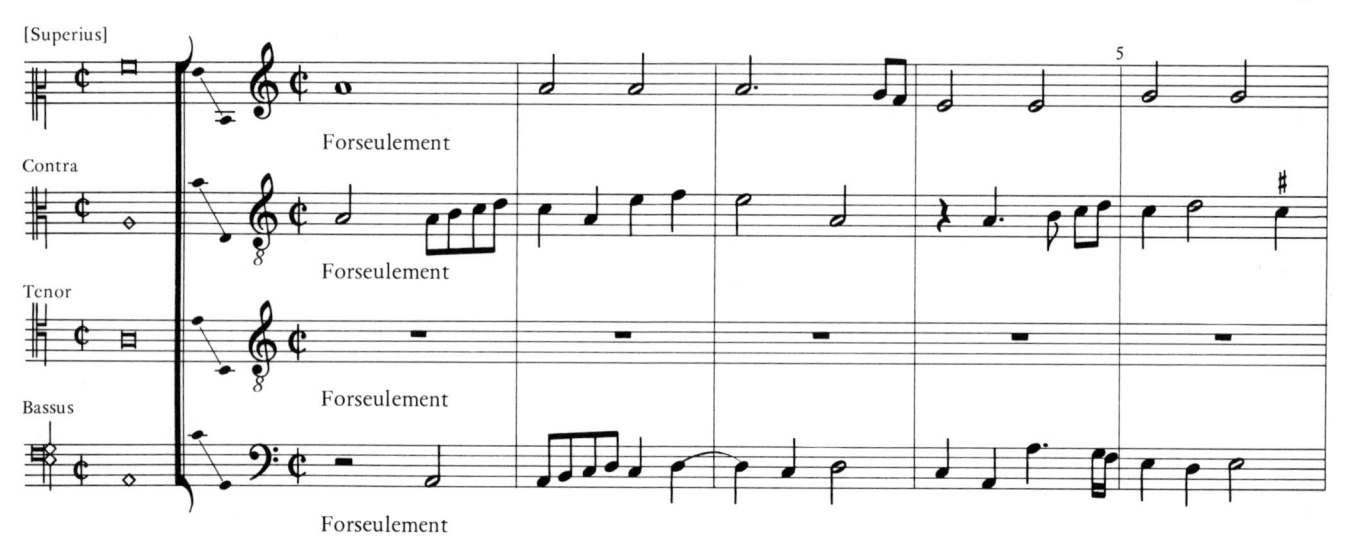

[Superius]
Forseulement

Contra
Forseulement

Tenor
Forseulement

Bassus
Forseulement

23

24

[8]

[Marbriano] de Orto

[Superius] Fors seullement

Contra Fors seullement

Tenor Fors seullement

Bassus Fors seullement

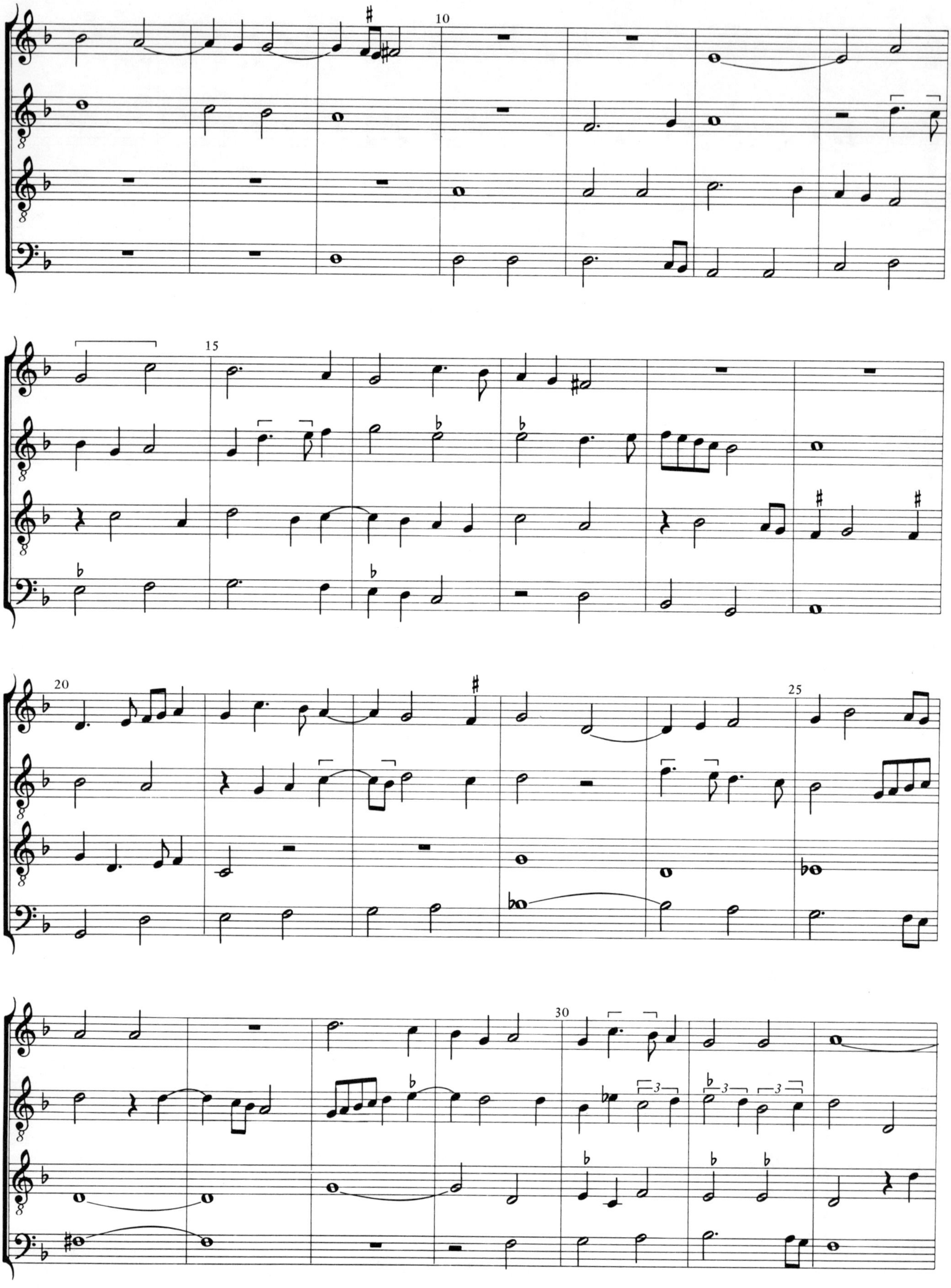
10
15
20
25
30

27

[9]

Jo[hannes] Agricola

Fors seulement

29

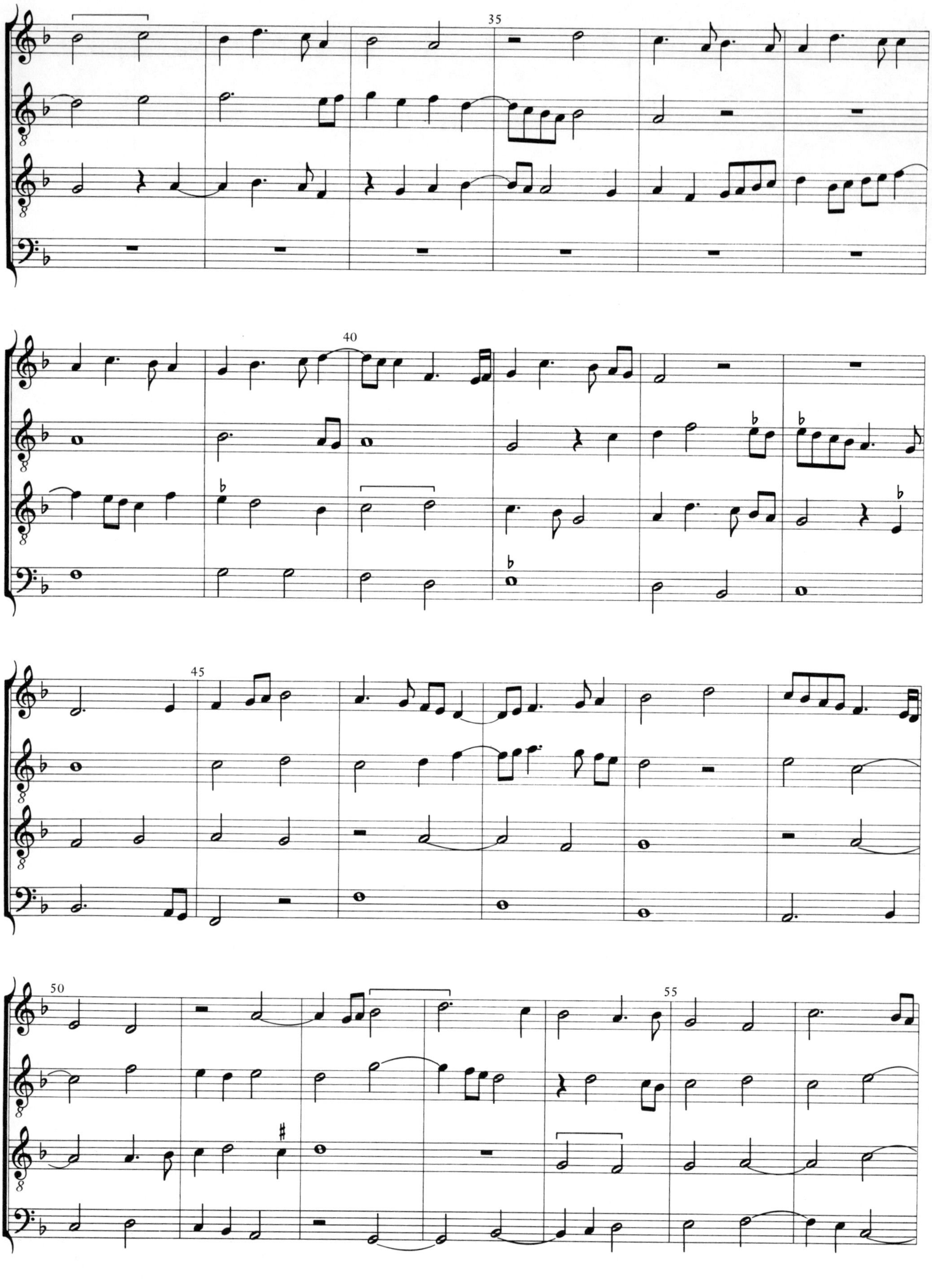

35
40
45
50
55

31

[10]

[Anonymous]

D[iscantus]

[Altus]

F[ors seullement]

T[enor]

[Bassus]

F[ors seullement]

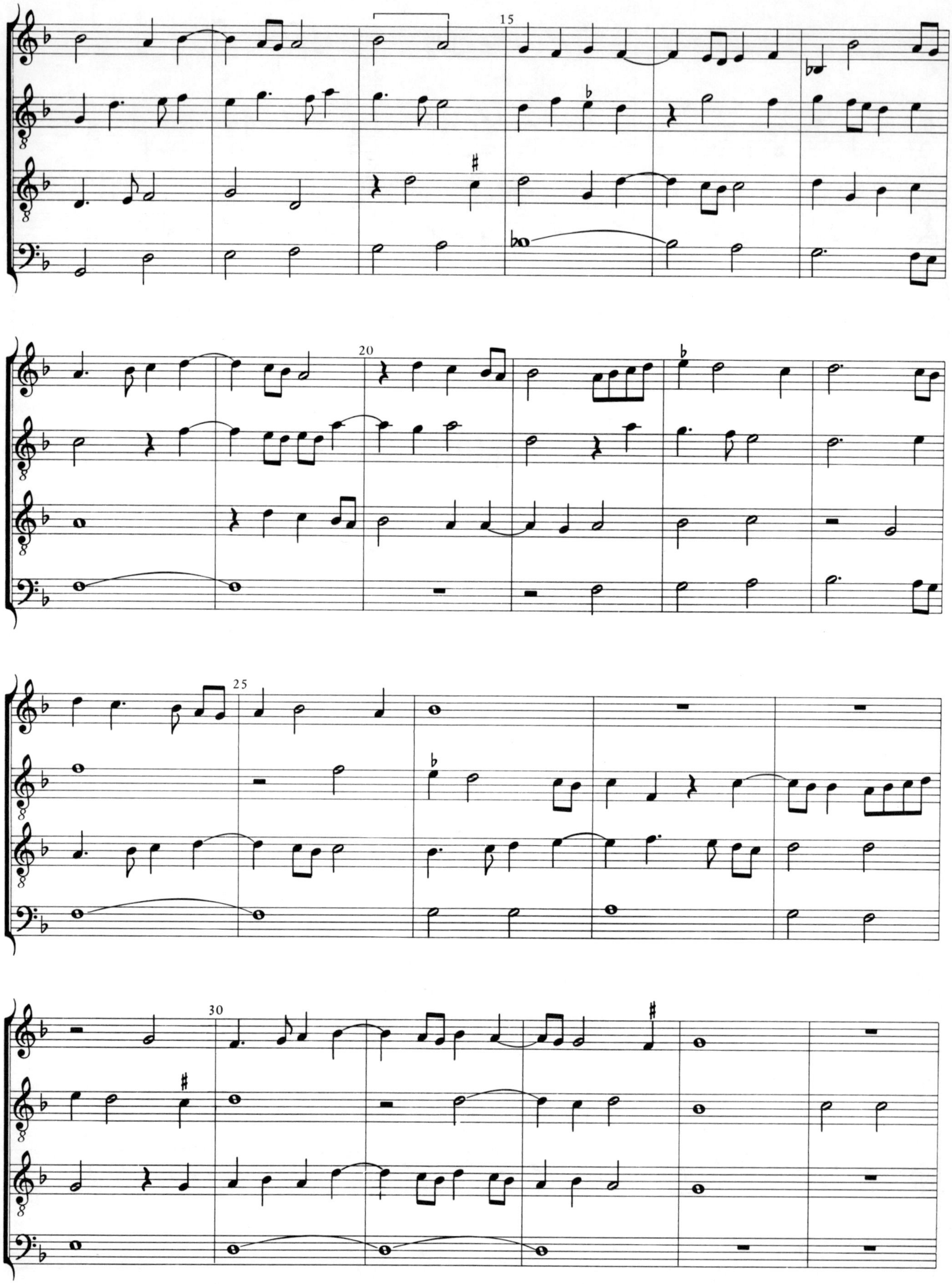
15
20
25
30

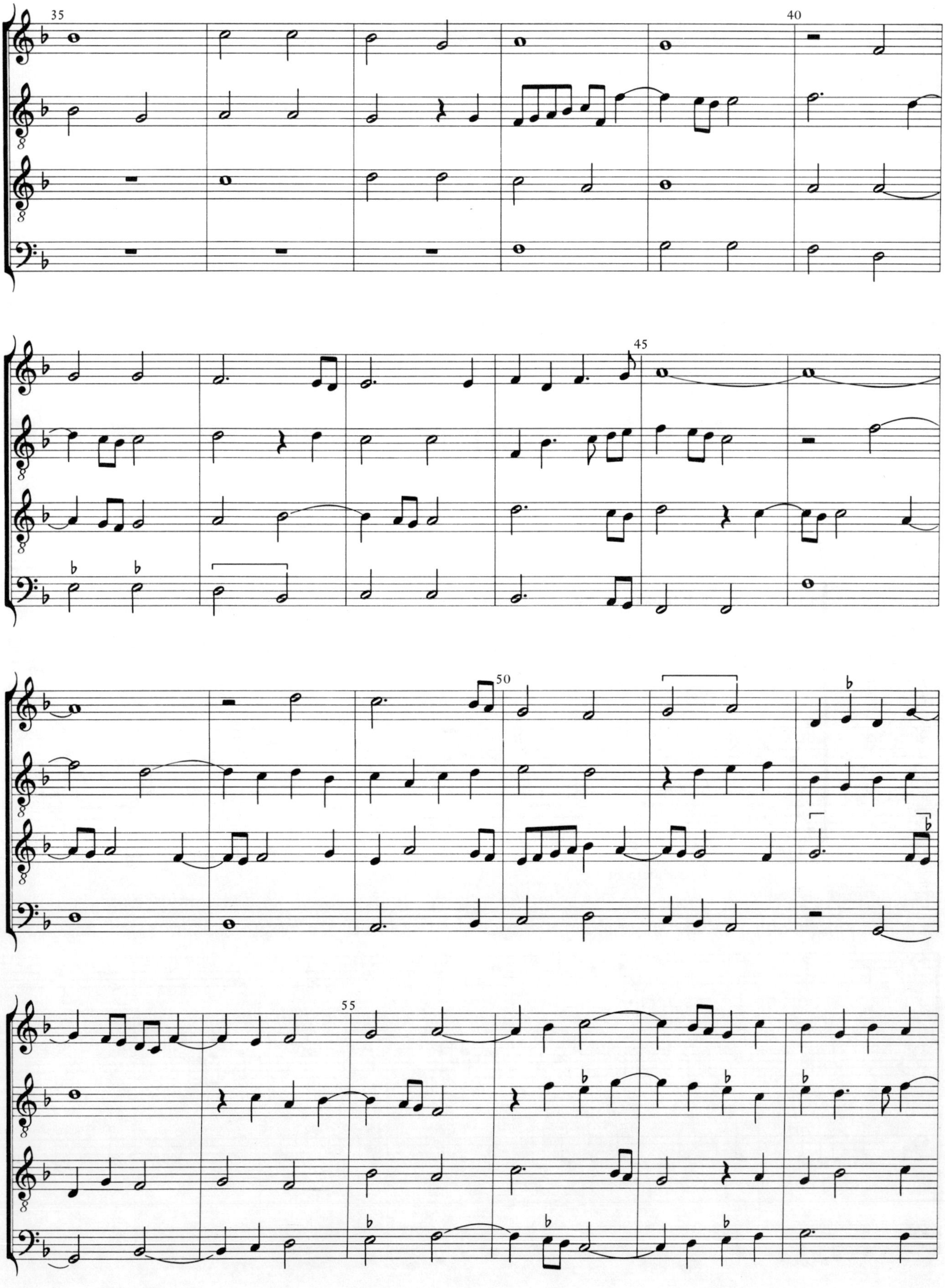
35
40
45
50
55

34

[11]

Andreas de Sylva

[Superius]

[Altus]

Fors seulement

[Tenor]

Fors seulement

[Bassus]

Fors seulement

Fors seulement

35

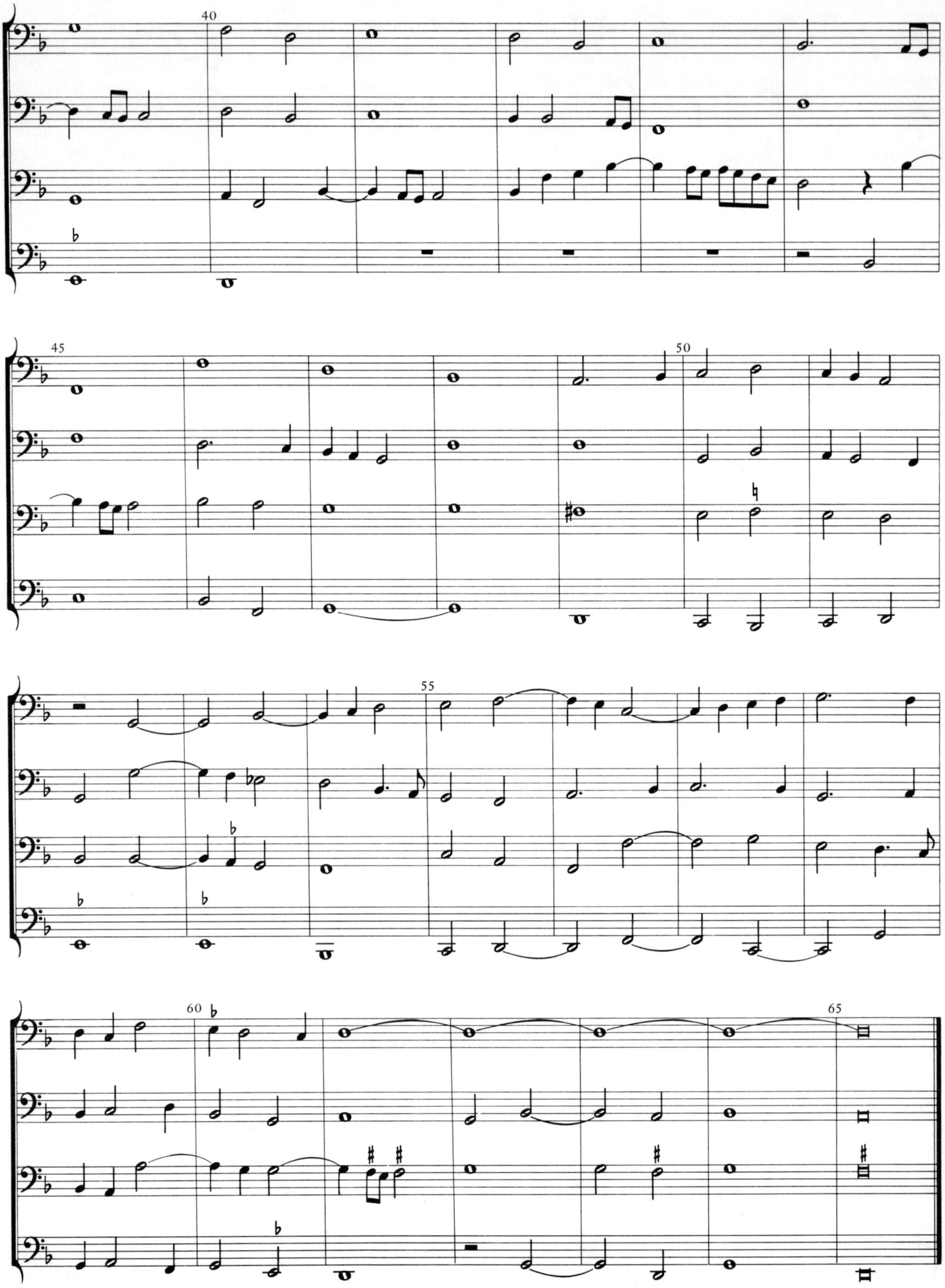
40
45
50
55
60
65

[12]

[Pierre de la] Rue

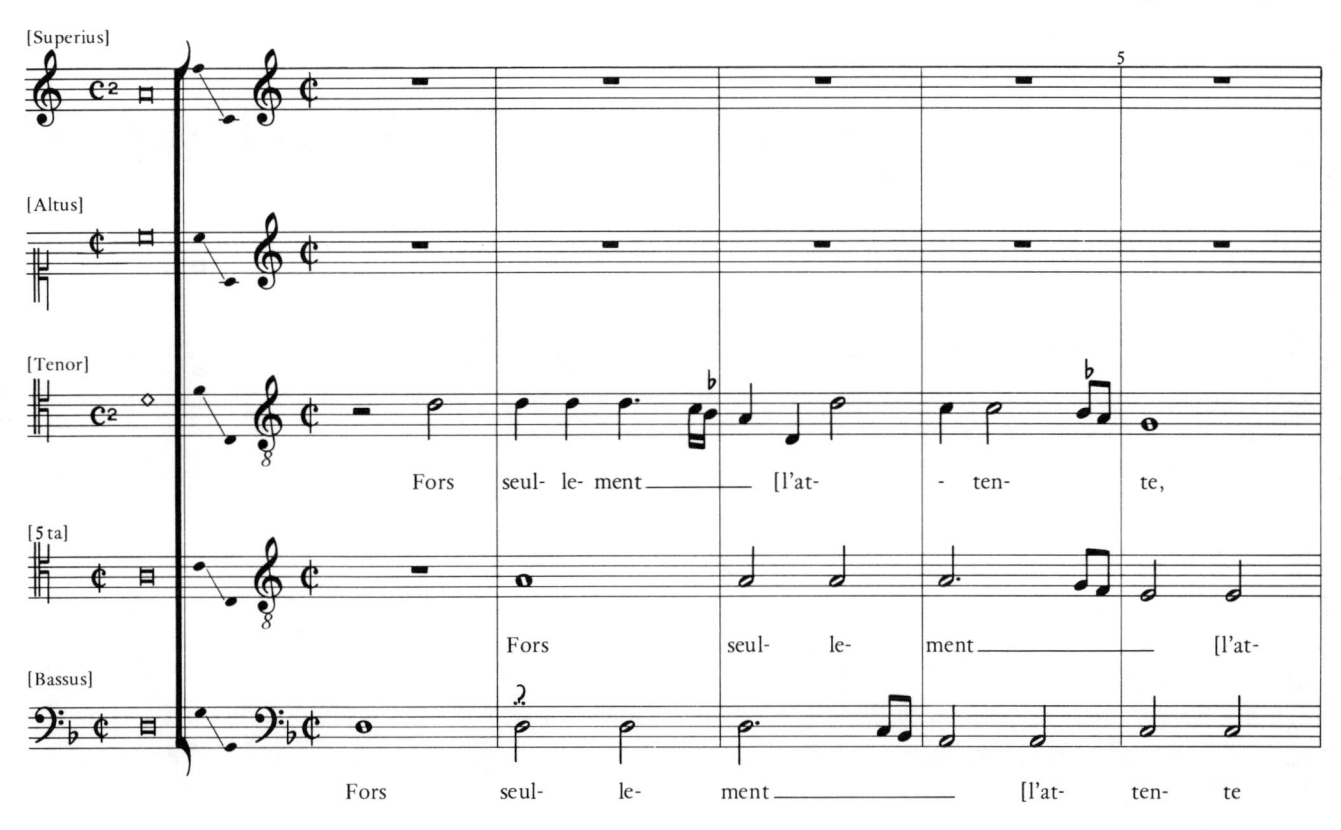

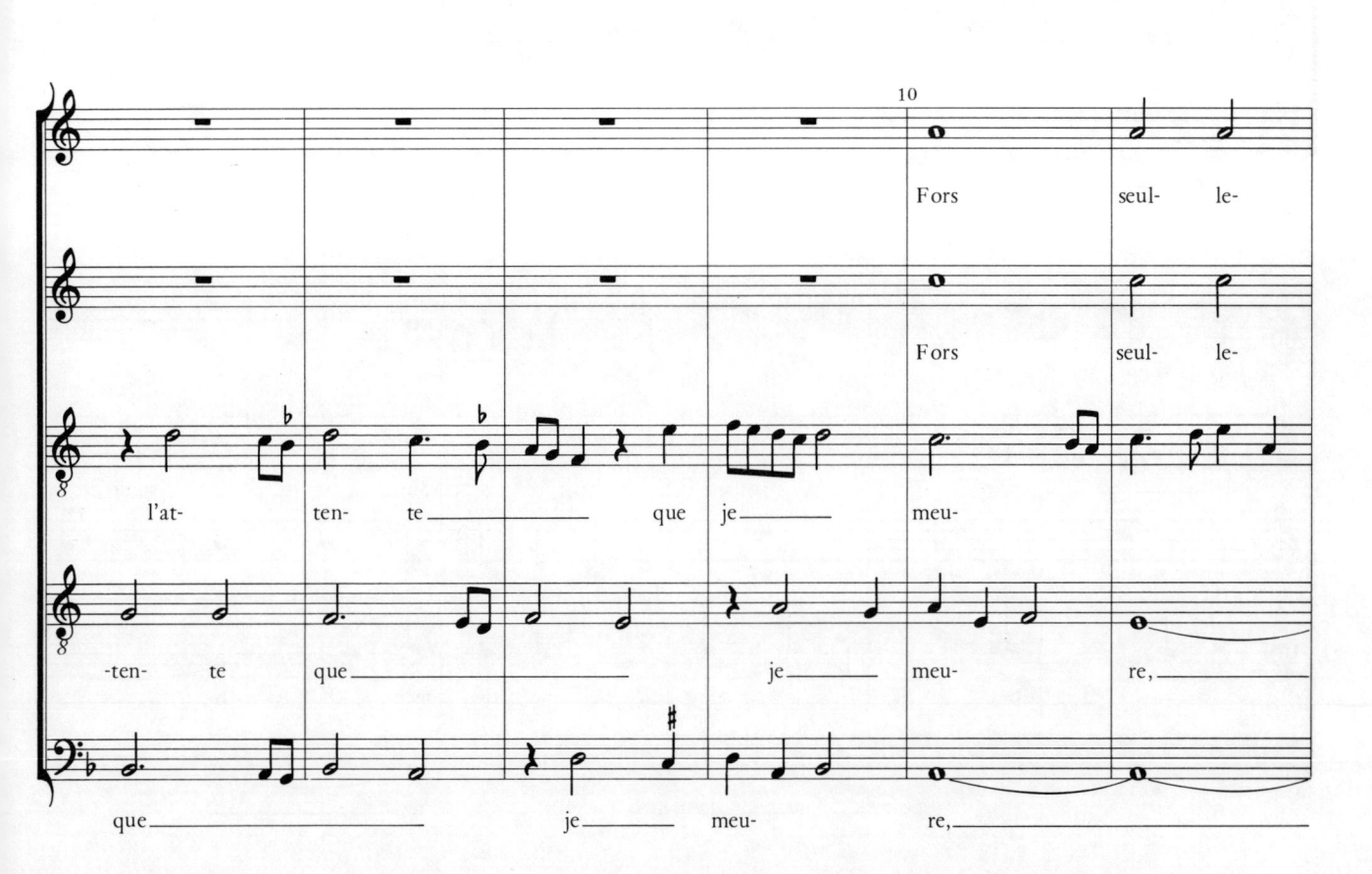

15
-ment [l'at- ten- te que je meu- re,
-ment [l'at- ten- - te que
-re, En mon las cueur nul e-
En mon las cueur
En mon las cueur nul e-
20
En mon las cueur nul e- spoir
je meu- - re, En mon
- spoir ne de- meu- -
nul e- spoir, nul
-spoir, nul
25
ne de- meu- - - re,
las cueur nul e- spoir
-re, Car mon mal- heur si
e- - spoir ne de- meu- re,
e- - spoir ne de- meu- re,

30
Car mon mal- heur
ne de- - meu- - re, Car
tres- - fort me tour- - men- te si
Car mon mal- heur si
Car mon mal- heur si tres-
35
si tres- fort me tour- men-
mon mal- heur si tres- fort
tres- - fort me
tres- fort, car mon mal- heur
-fort, car mon mal- heur si tres- fort
40
-te]
me tour- - - men- te
tour- - - - men- te
si tres- fort me tour- - - men- te
me tour- - men- te

45
Qu'il n'est dou- leur que par
Qu'il n'est dou- leur que par vous,
Qu'il n'est dou- - leur que par
Qu'il n'est dou- - leur que par vous,
50
55
Qu'il n'est dou- leur [que par vous je ne sen-
vous je ne sen- - te, que par vous
qu'il n'est dou- leur que par
vous, vous, par vous
vous, par vous je ne
60
-te Pour- ce que suis
je ne sen- te
vous je ne sen-
je ne sen- te Pour- ce
sen- te Pour- ce que

65
de vous per- - dre
Pour- ce que suis de vous per-
-te Pour- ce que suis de vous
que suis de
suis de vous
70
bien seu-
-dre bien
per- dre bien
vous per- - - dre
per- - - dre
75
- - re.]
seu- - re.]
seu- re.]
bien, bien seu- re.]
bien, bien seu- re.]

[13]

[Anonymous]

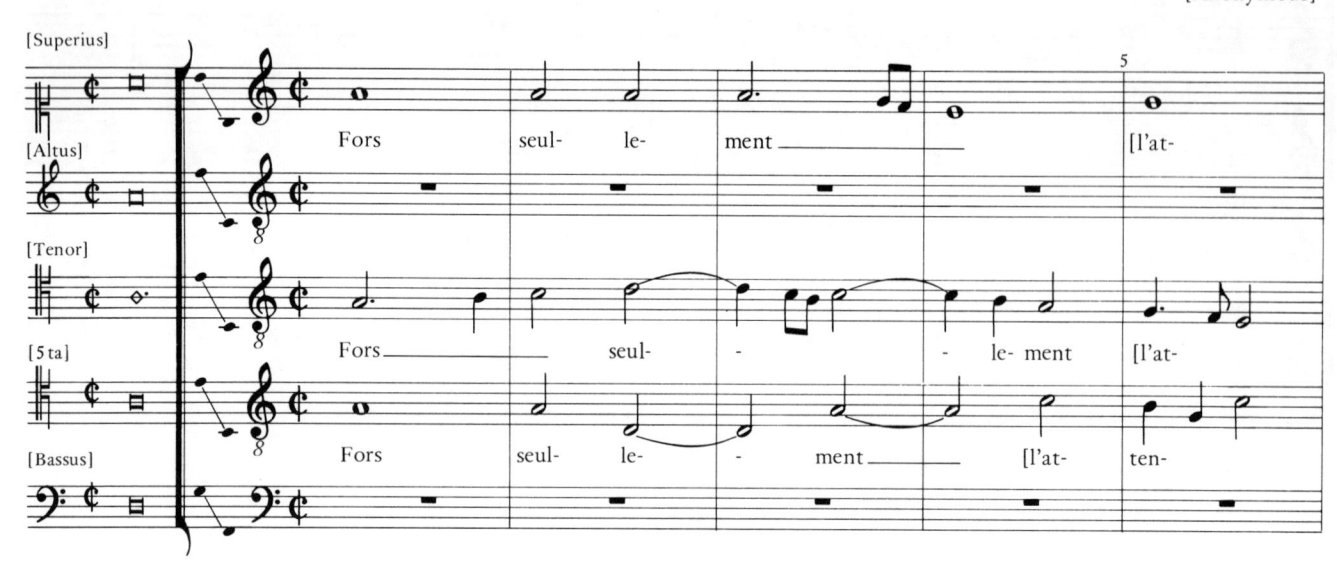

20
mon las cueur nul e- spoir ne de- meu- re,
mon las cueur nul e- spoir ne
las cueur nul e- spoir ne de- meu- - re, ne
En mon las cueur nul e- spoir, nul e- spoir
seul- le- ment l'at- ten- te que
25
nul e- spoir ne de- meu- re,
de- meu- re,
de- meu- re, Car mon mal- heur si tres- fort me tour- men-
ne de- meu- re,
je meu- re, Car mon mal- heur si tres-
30
Car mon mal- heur, car mon mal- heur
Car mon mal- heur
- - - te, Car mon mal- heur si
Car mon mal- heur, car mon mal-
- fort me tour- men- te, me tour- men- te,

35
si tres- fort me tour- men- te
si tres- fort me tour- men- te
tres- fort me tour- - men- -
-heur si tres- fort, si tres-
Car mon mal- heur si
40
-te, si tres- fort me tour- men- te
-fort me tour- - men- - te
tres- fort me tour- men- te, si tres- fort me tour- men- te
45
Qu'il n'est
Qu'il n'est dou- leur que par vous
Qu'il n'est dou- leur que par
Qu'il n'est dou- leur, qu'il n'est dou- leur

50
dou- leur que par vous,
Qu'il n'est dou- leur que par vous je
je ne sen- te, que par
vous je ne
que par
55
qu'il n'est dou- leur que par vous je ne sen-
ne sen- te Pour- ce
vous, Qu'il n'est dou- leur que par vous je ne sen-
sen- te, je ne sen- te, je ne, je
vous je ne
60
te Pour- ce
que suis de vous per-
- te Pour- ce
ne sen- te Pour- ce
sen- te Pour- ce que suis de vous per- - dre

65
que suis, pour- ce que suis de vous,
70
- dre bien seu-
que suis de vous per- - dre bien
que suis de vous per- dre bien seu-
bien seu- - - re,
75
de vous per- dre bien seu- re, de vous
- - re.]
seu- - re, de vous per-
- - re, Pour- ce que suis de vous per- - dre,
Pour- ce que suis de vous,
80
per- dre bien seu- re, de vous per- dre bien seu- re.]
-dre bien seu- re, bien seu- re.]
per- dre bien seu- re.]
pour- ce que suis de vous bien seu- re.]

[14]

[Anonymous]

Fors seullement [l'at- ten- te que je meu- re, En mon las cueur nul e- spoir ne de- meu- re,

48

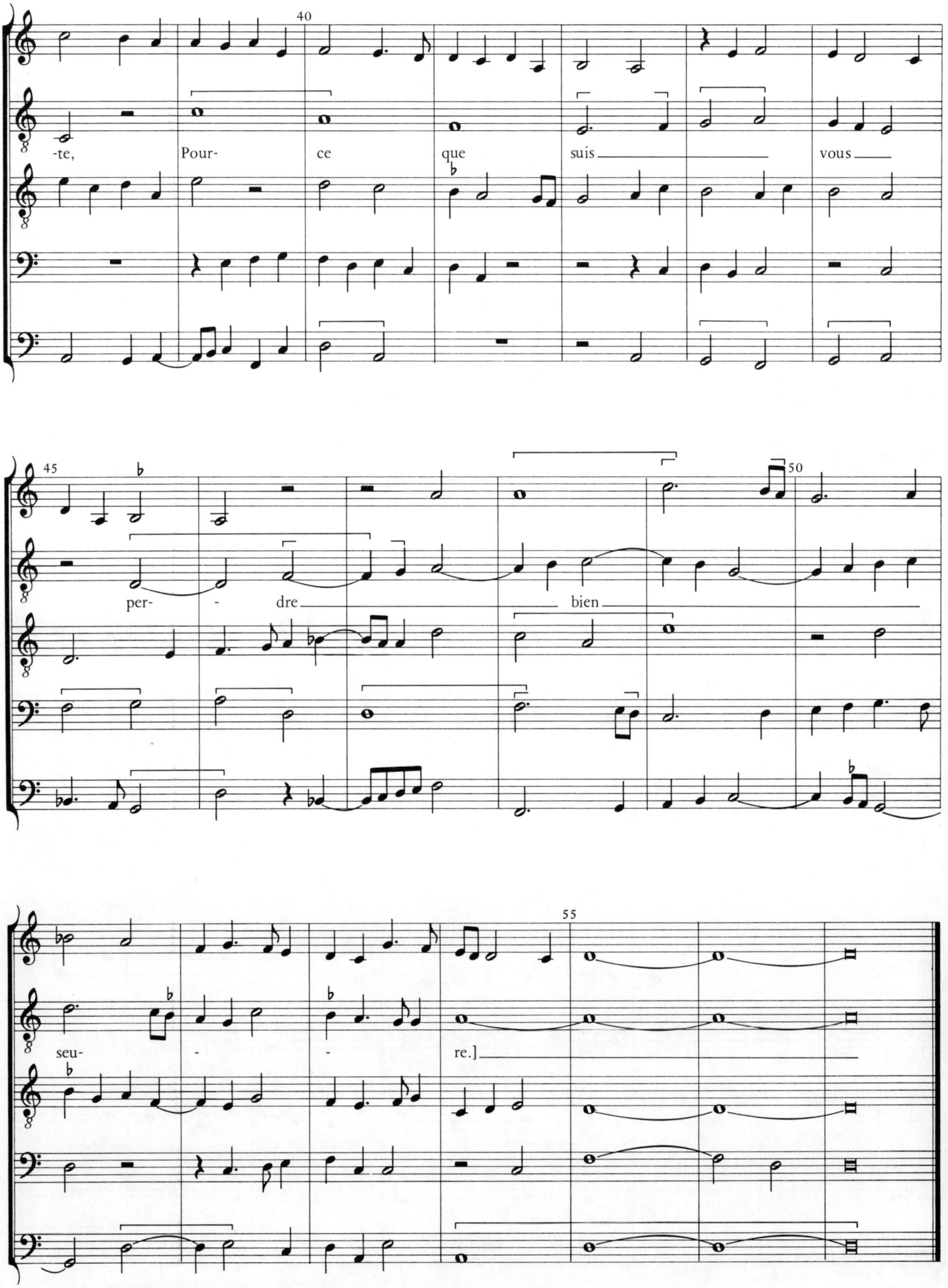
40
-te, Pour- ce que suis vous
45
50
per- - dre bien
55
seu- - - re.]

[15]

[Anonymous]

[Superius] Fors seullement

[Altus] Fors seullement

[Tenor] Fors seullement

[5 ta] Fors seullement

[Bassus] Fors seullement

51

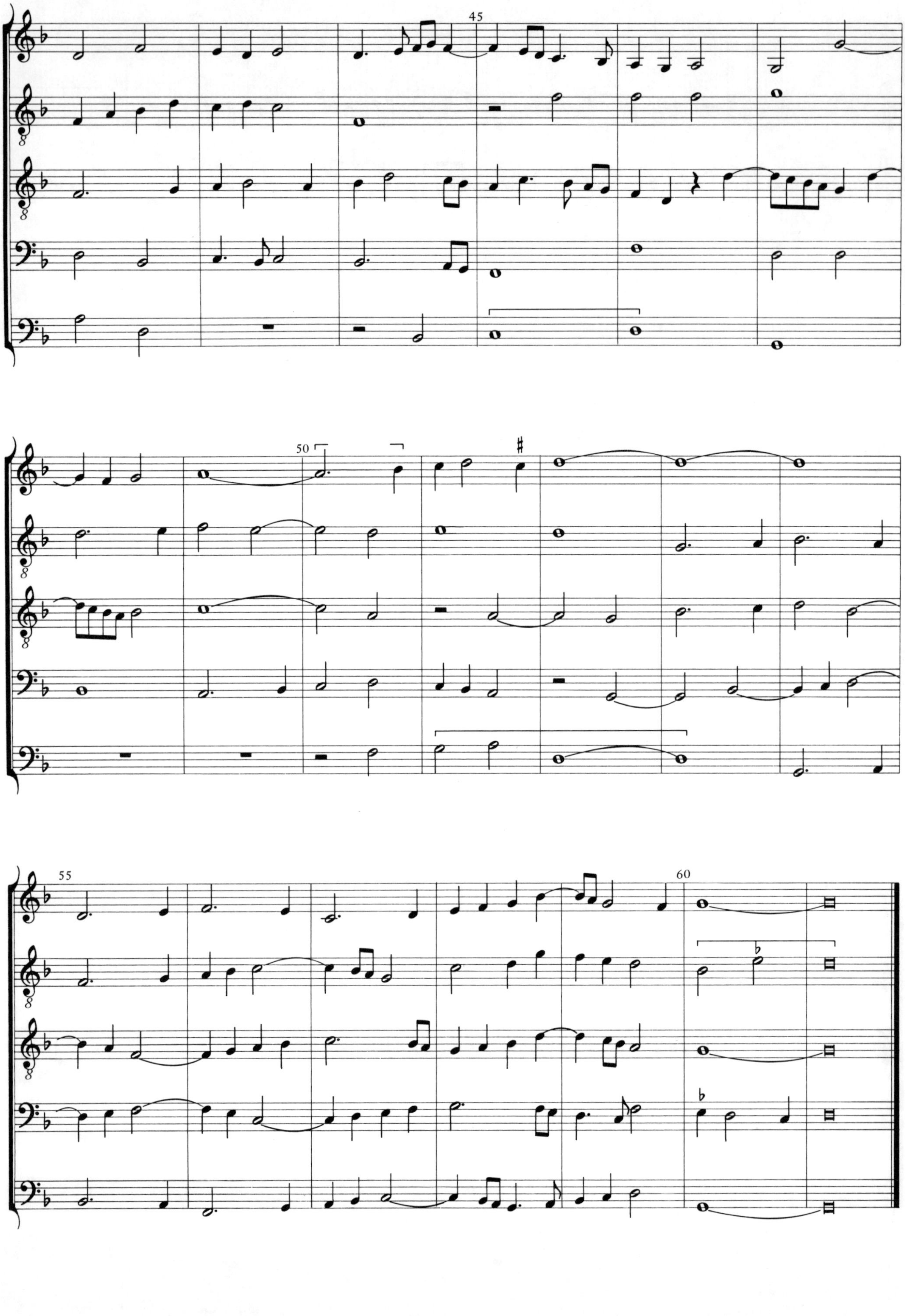
45
50
55
60

[16]

[Anonymous]

Fors seullement

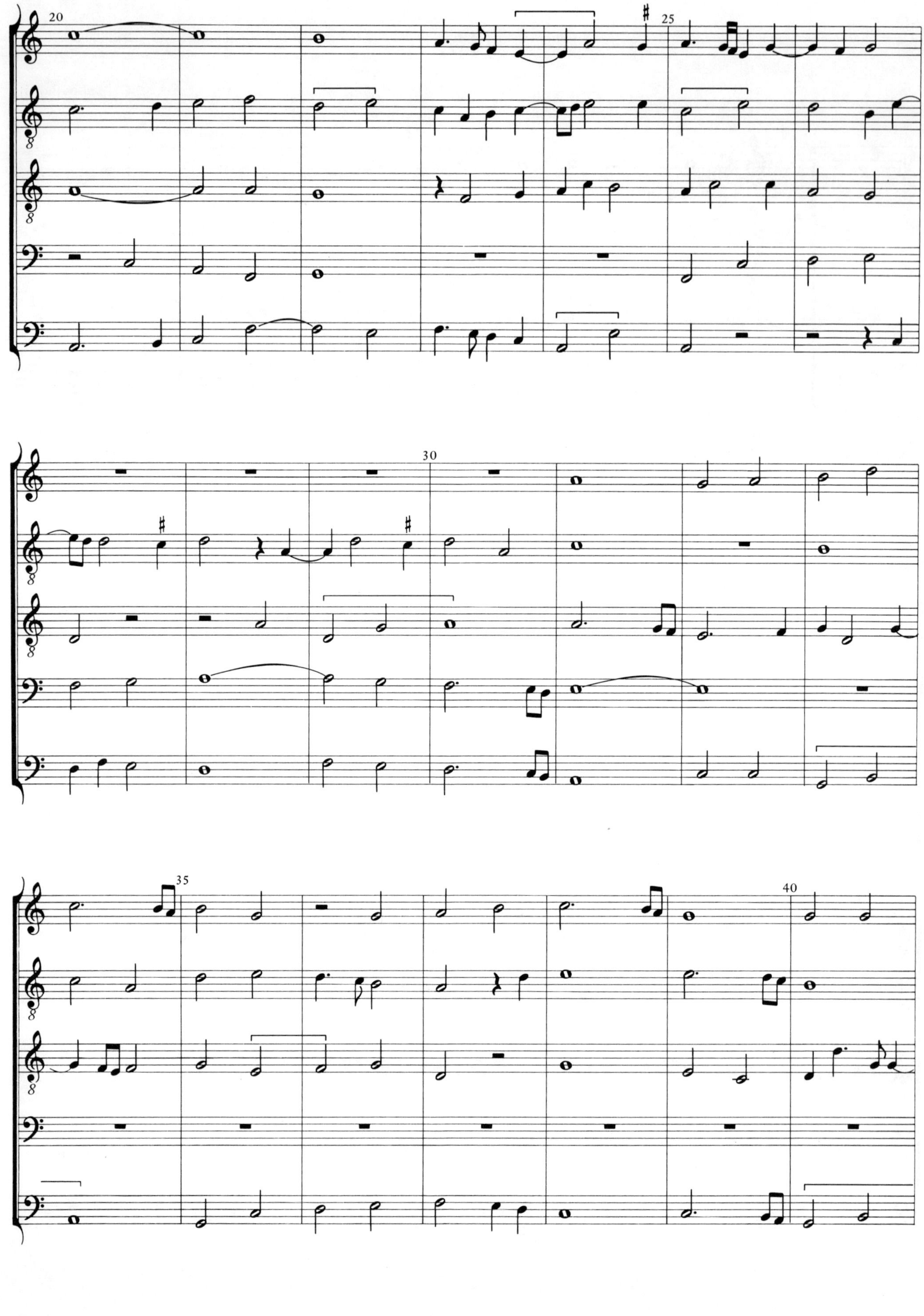
20
25
30
35
40

55

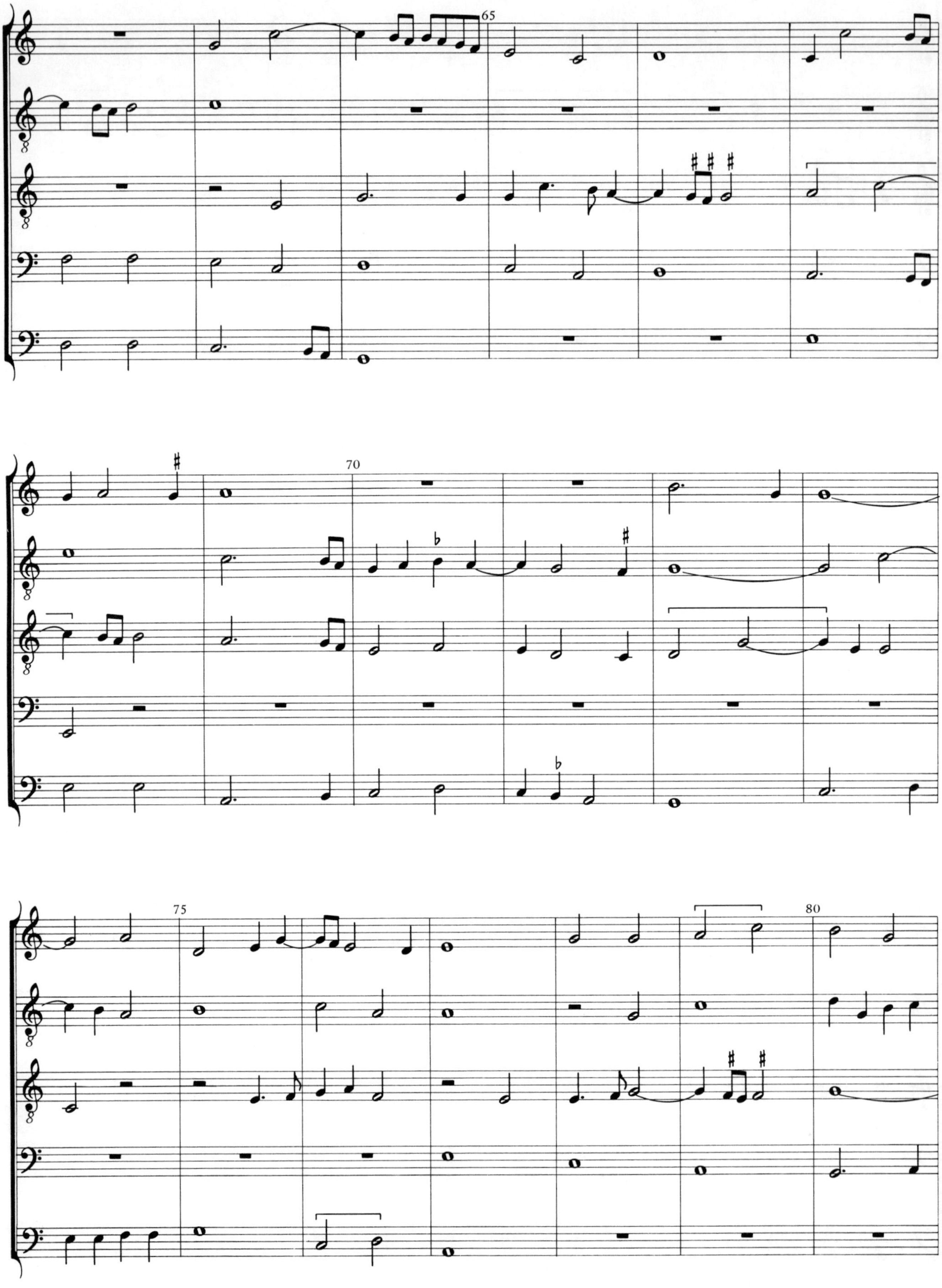
65
70
75
80

57

[17]

Antonius Divitis

Fours seullement

Fours seullement l'etente que ie meur [...]

Fours seullement

Fours seullement

Fours seullement

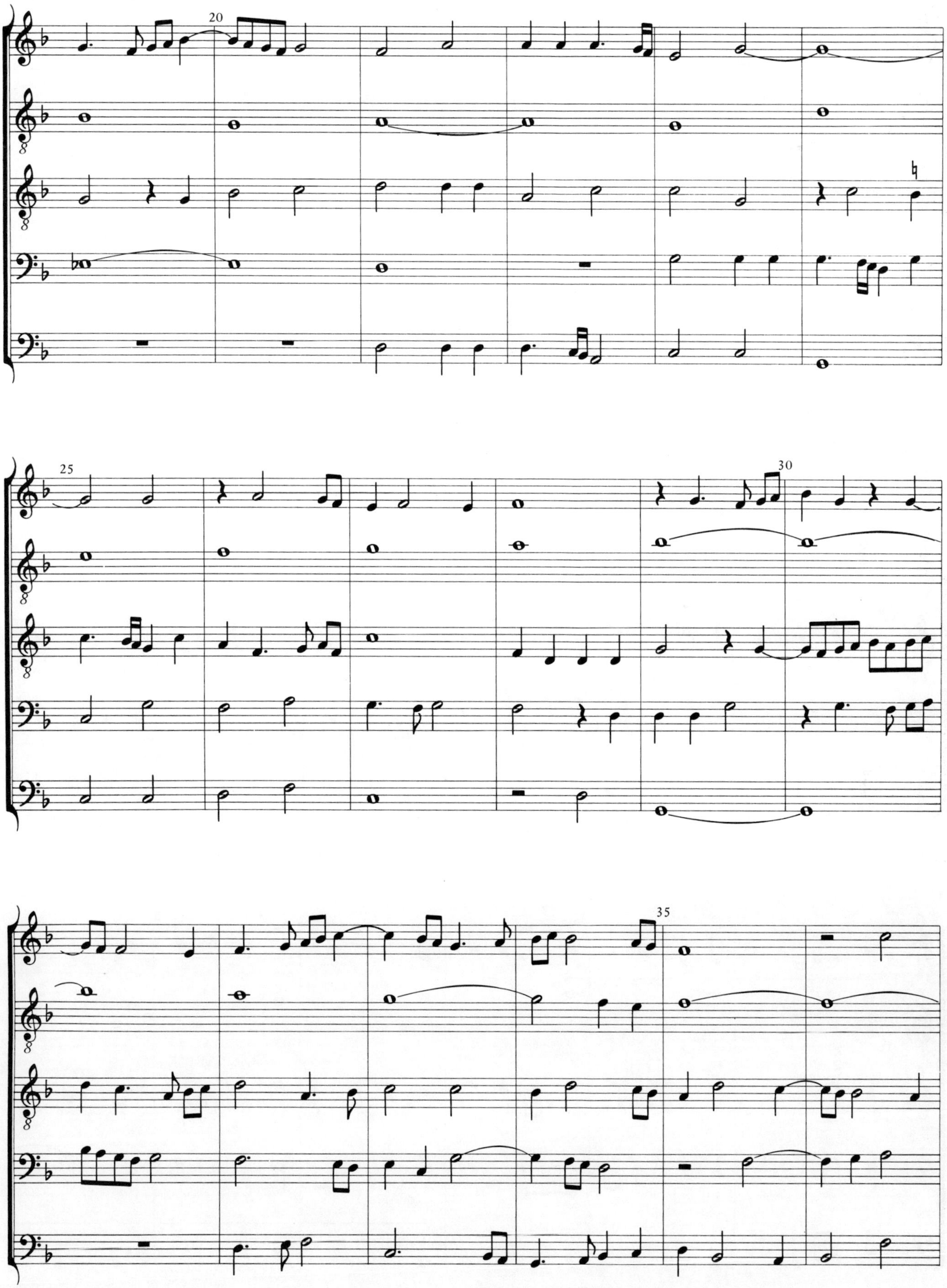
20
25
30
35

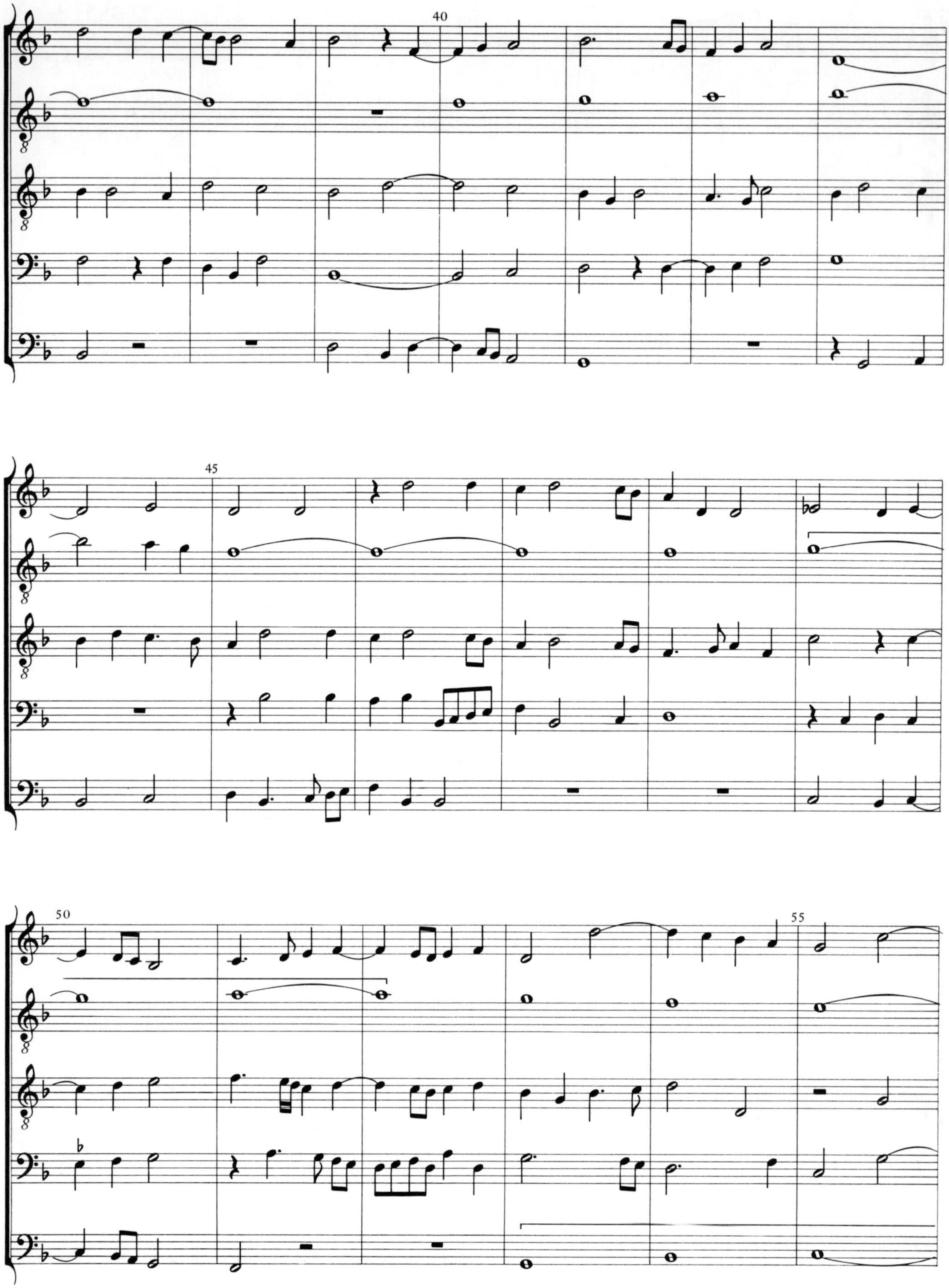
40
45
50
55

61

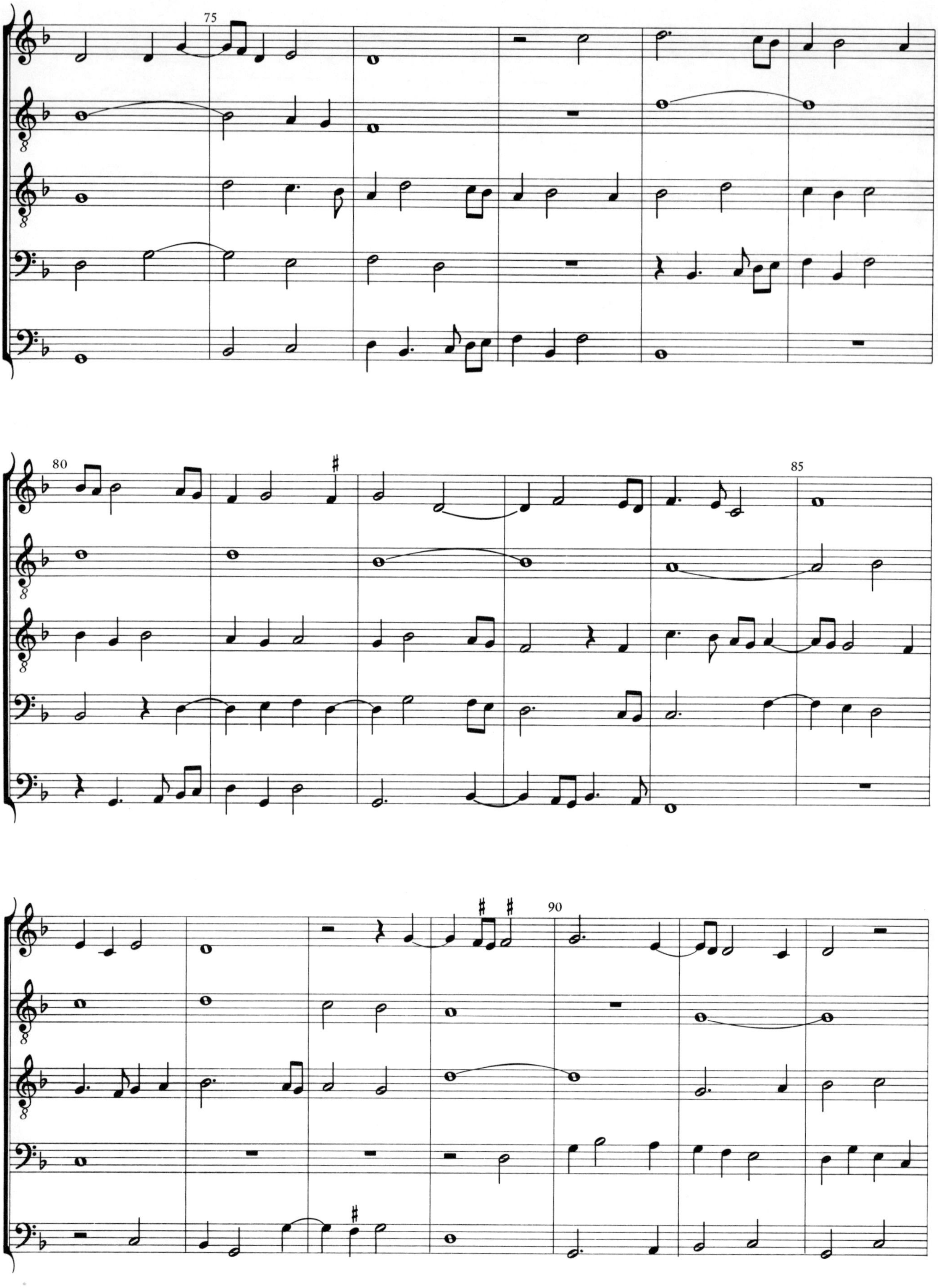
75
80
85
90

63

[18]

Jacob[us] Roman[us]

65

-leur que par vous je ne sen- te Pour-ce que suis de vous, pour-ce que suis de vous per- dre, pour-ce que suis de vous per- dre bien seu- -re.]

[19]

De la Val

[Superius]

[Altus] Fors seulement

[Tenor] Fors seulement

[Bassus]

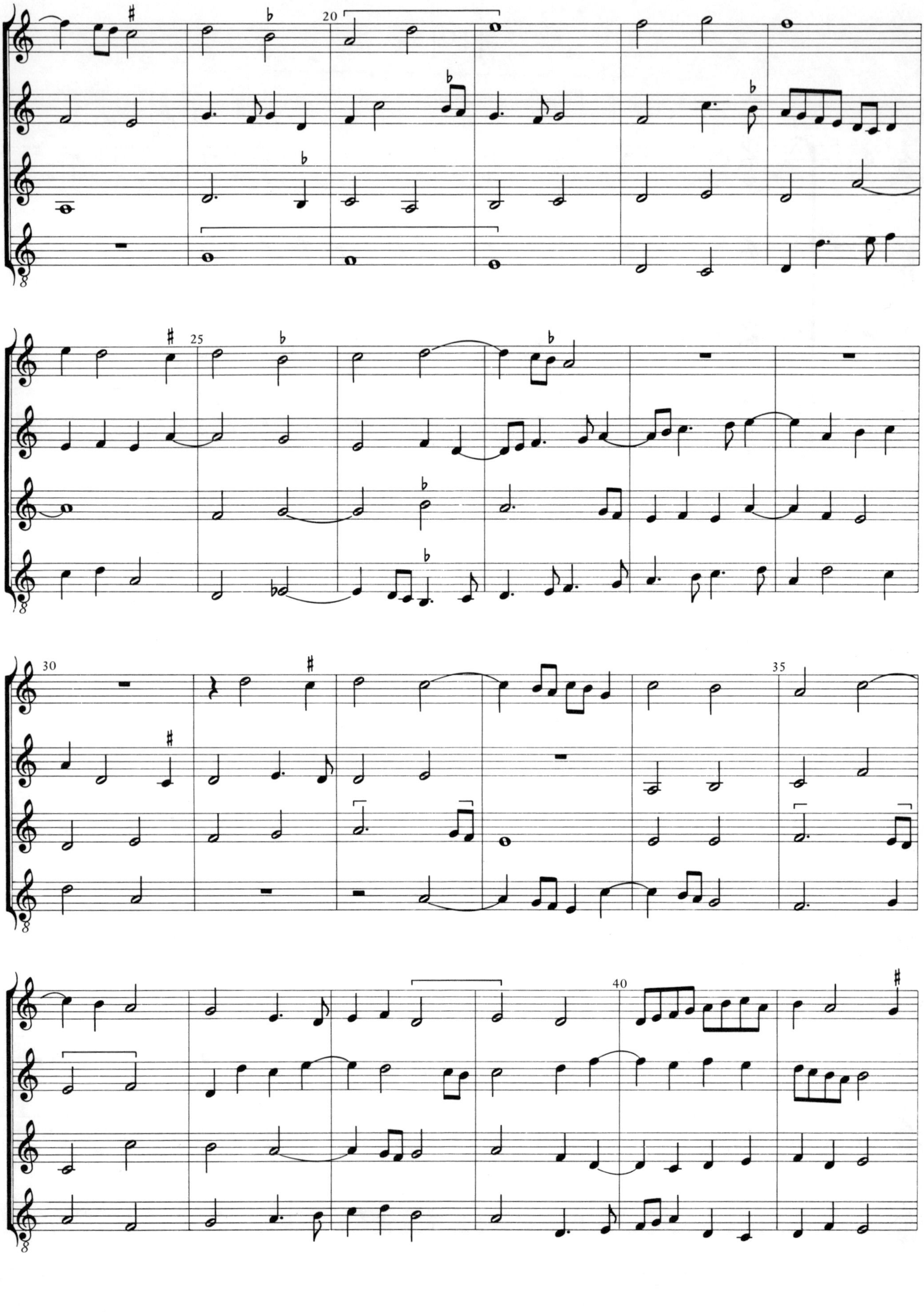

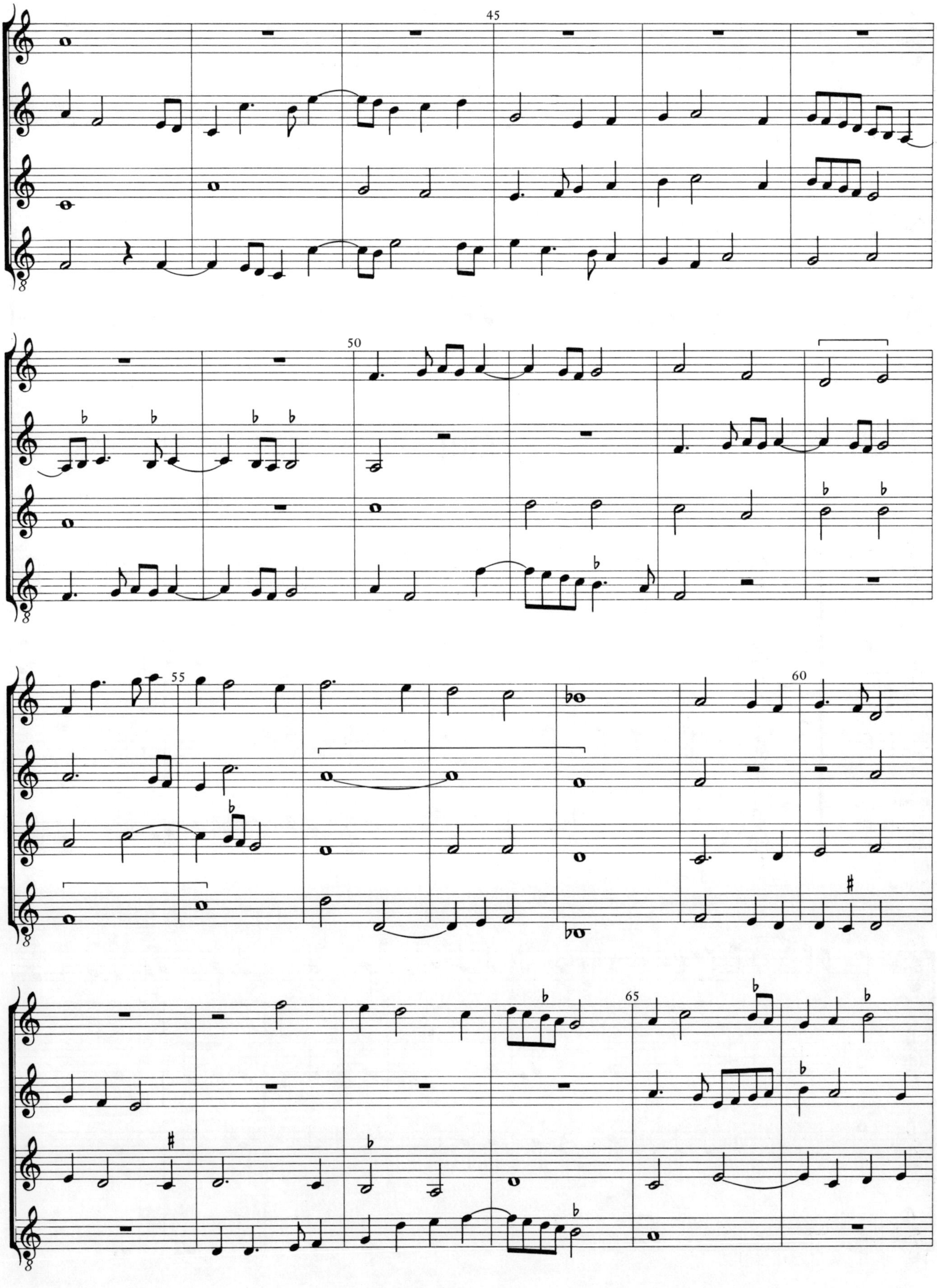
45
50
55
60
65

[20]

[Johannes] Ghisling [Verbonet]

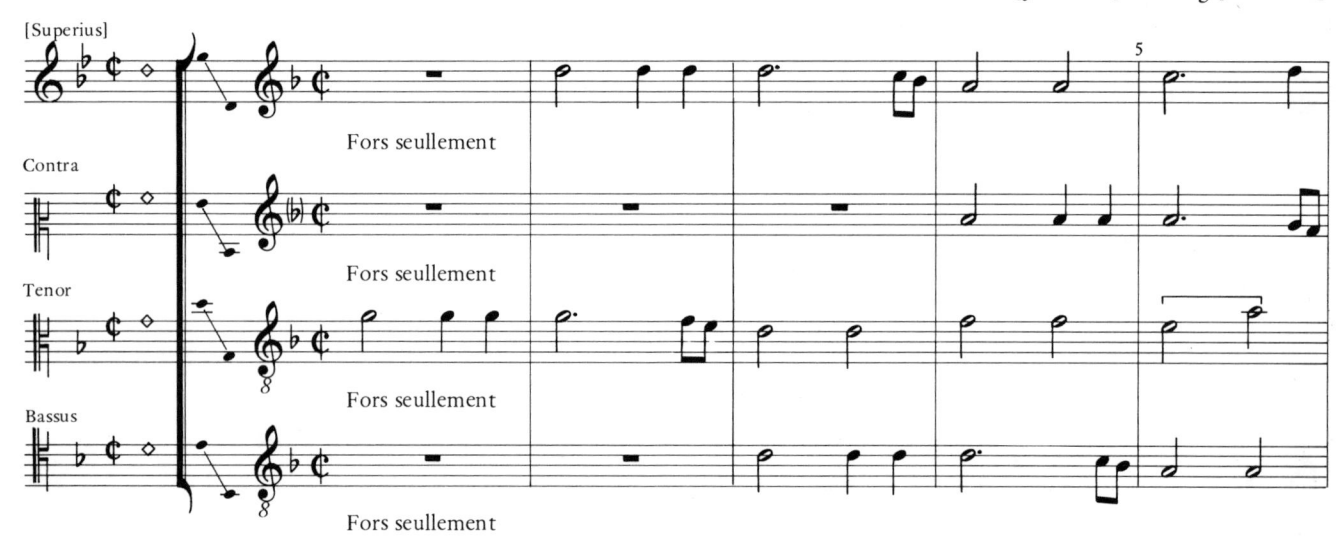

[Superius]

Fors seullement

Contra

Fors seullement

Tenor

Fors seullement

Bassus

Fors seullement

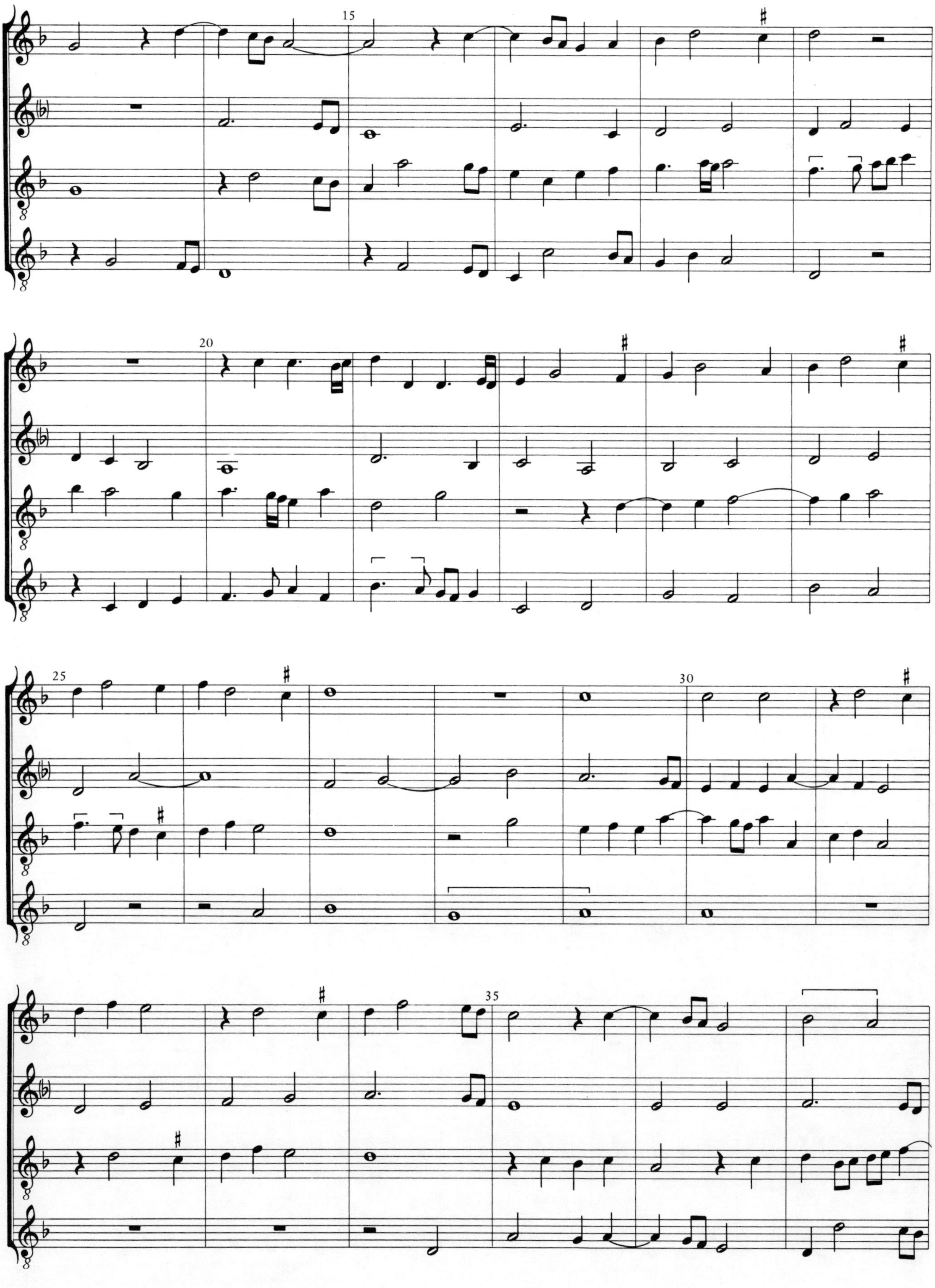
15
20
25
30
35

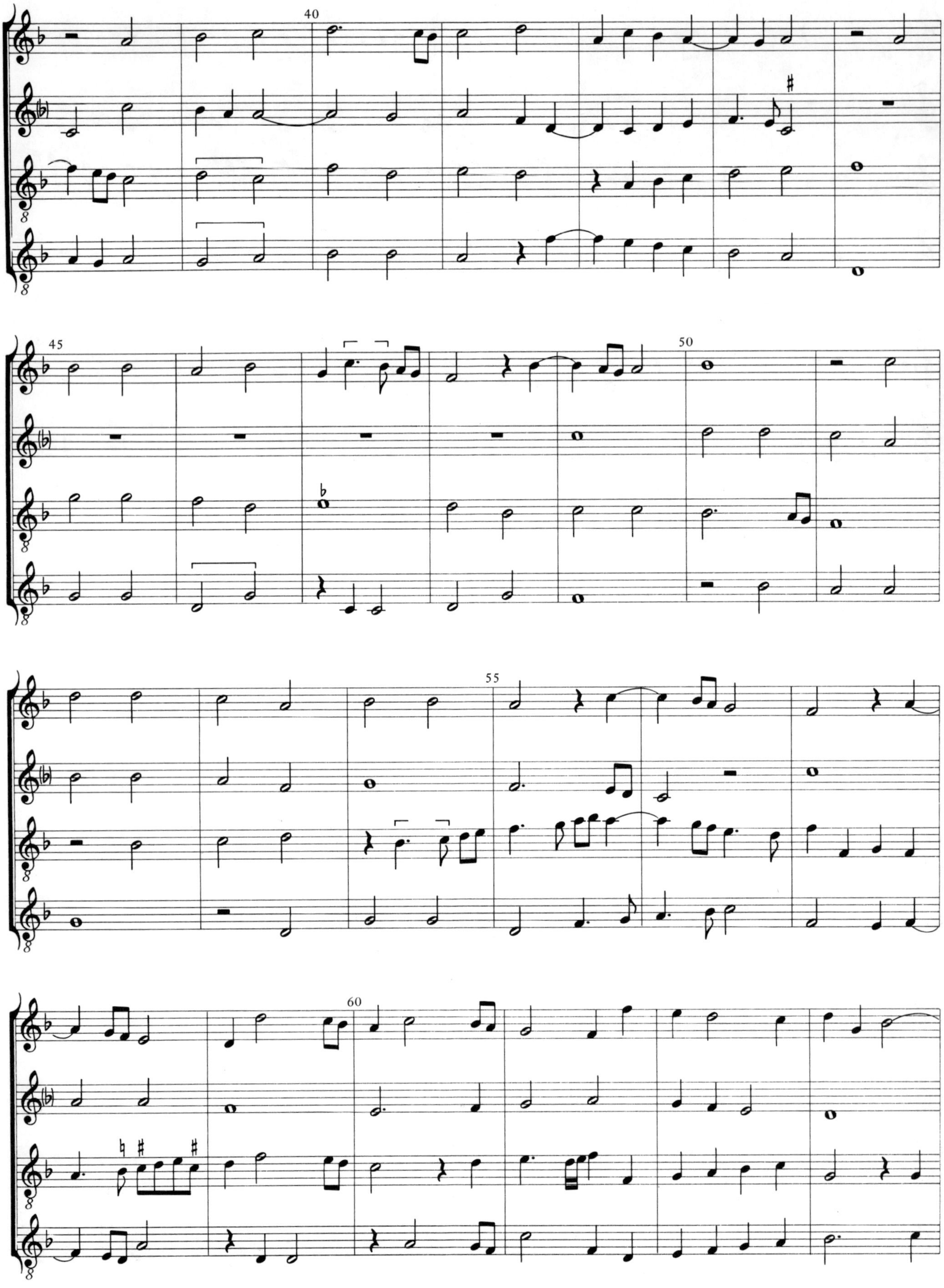
40
45
50
55
60

[21]

F[ors seulement]

[Incertus]

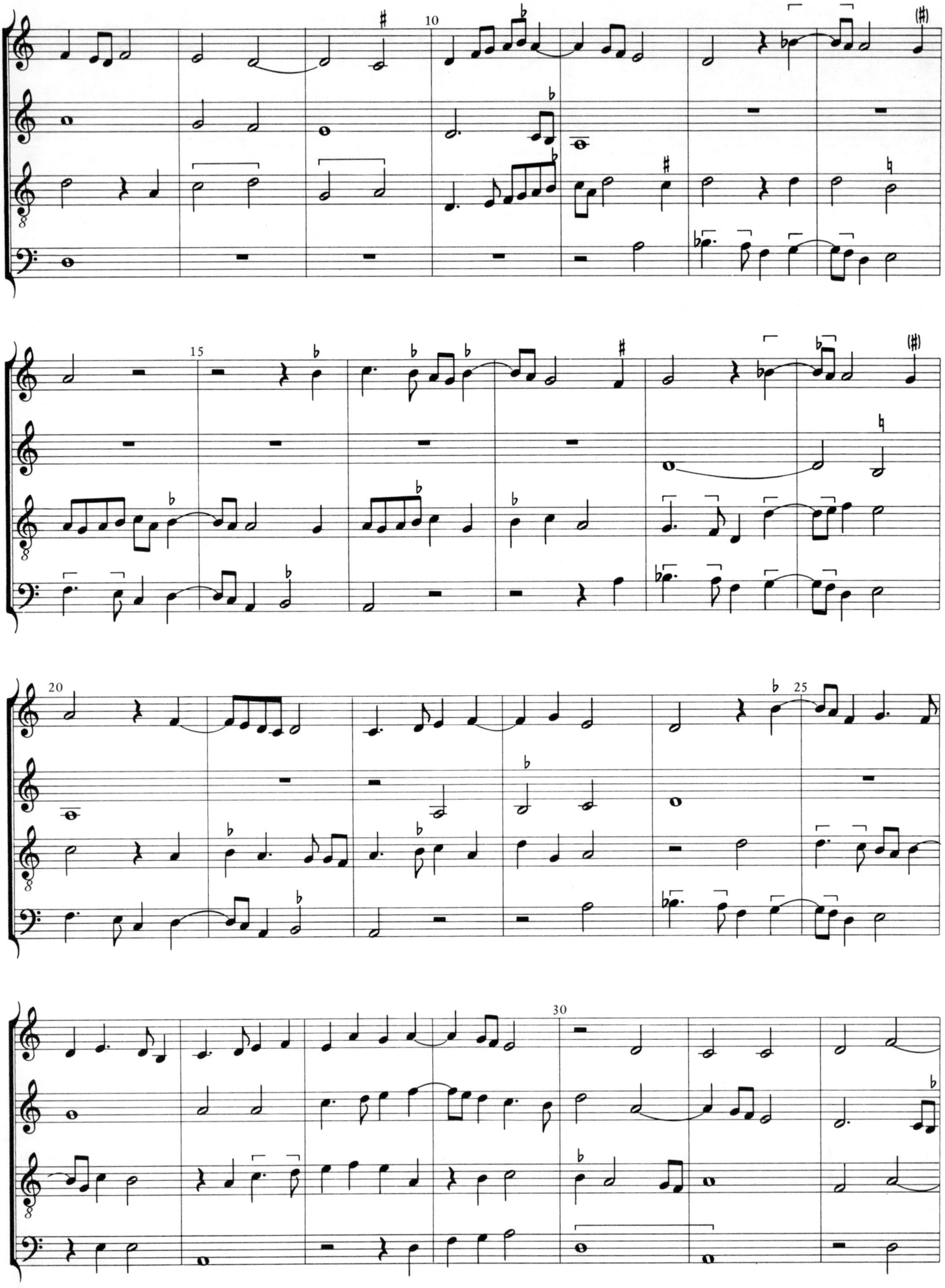

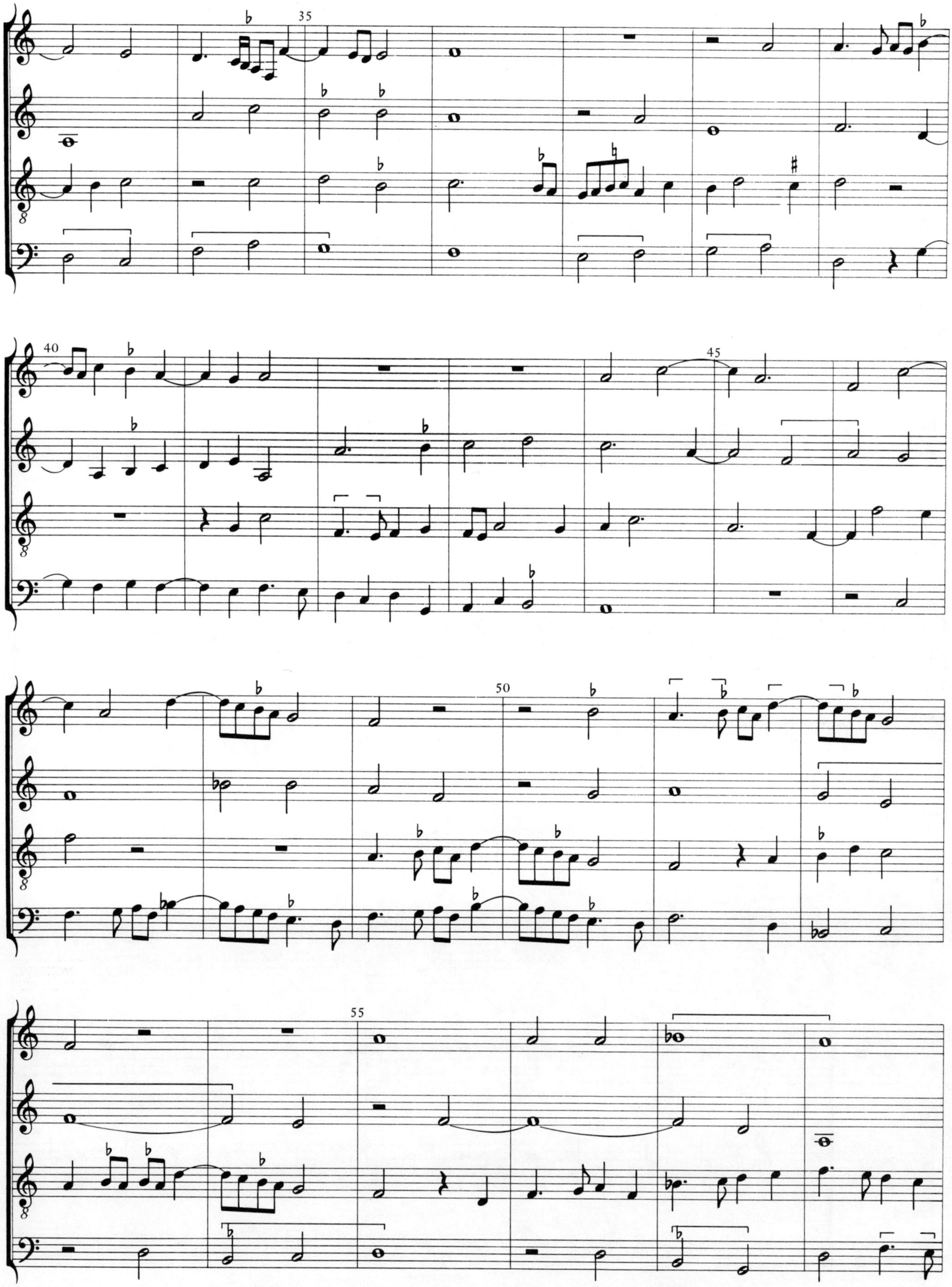

[22]

[Josquin des Prez?]

Fors seullement

77

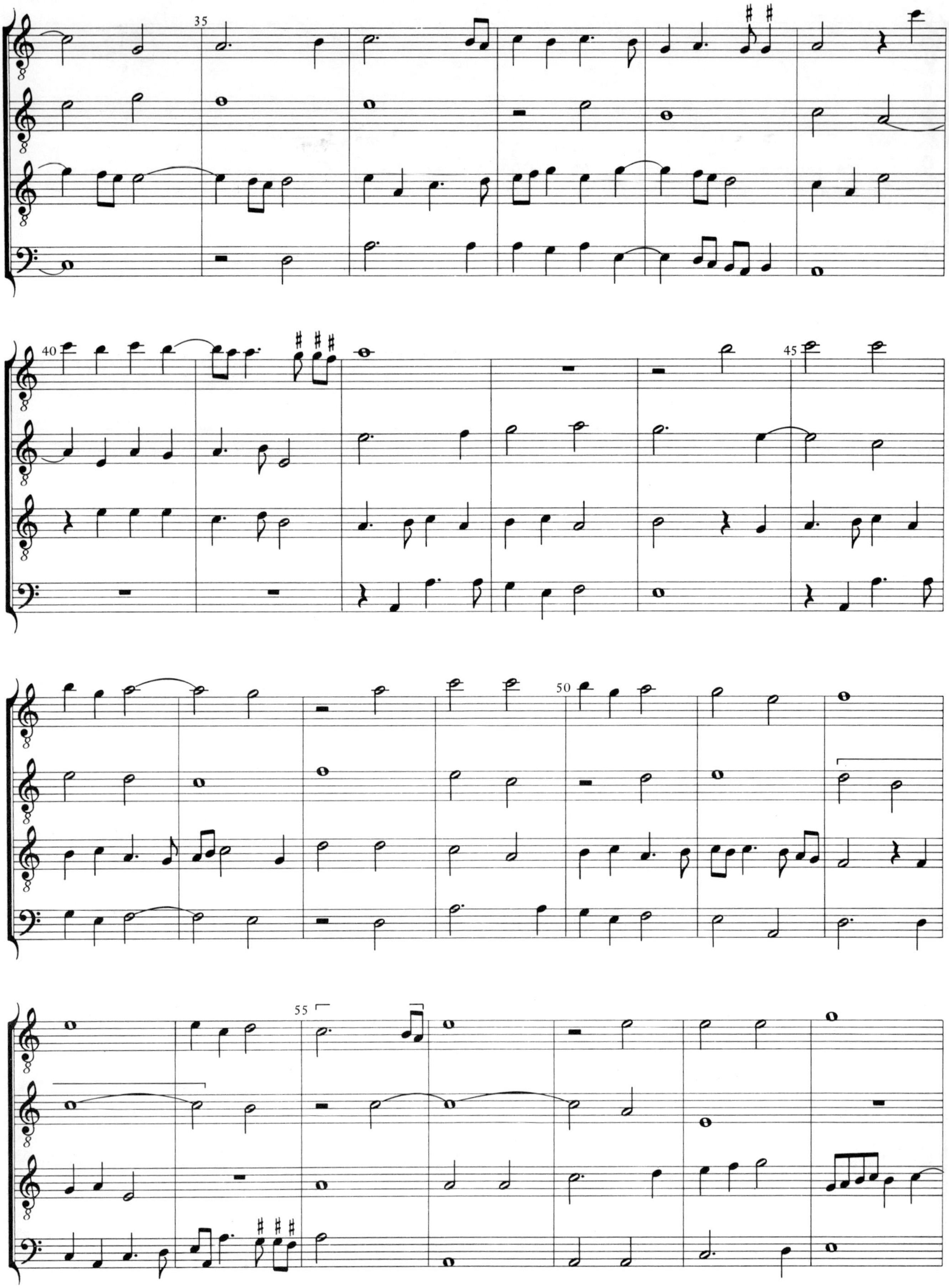
35
40
45
50
55

79

[23]

[Anonymous]

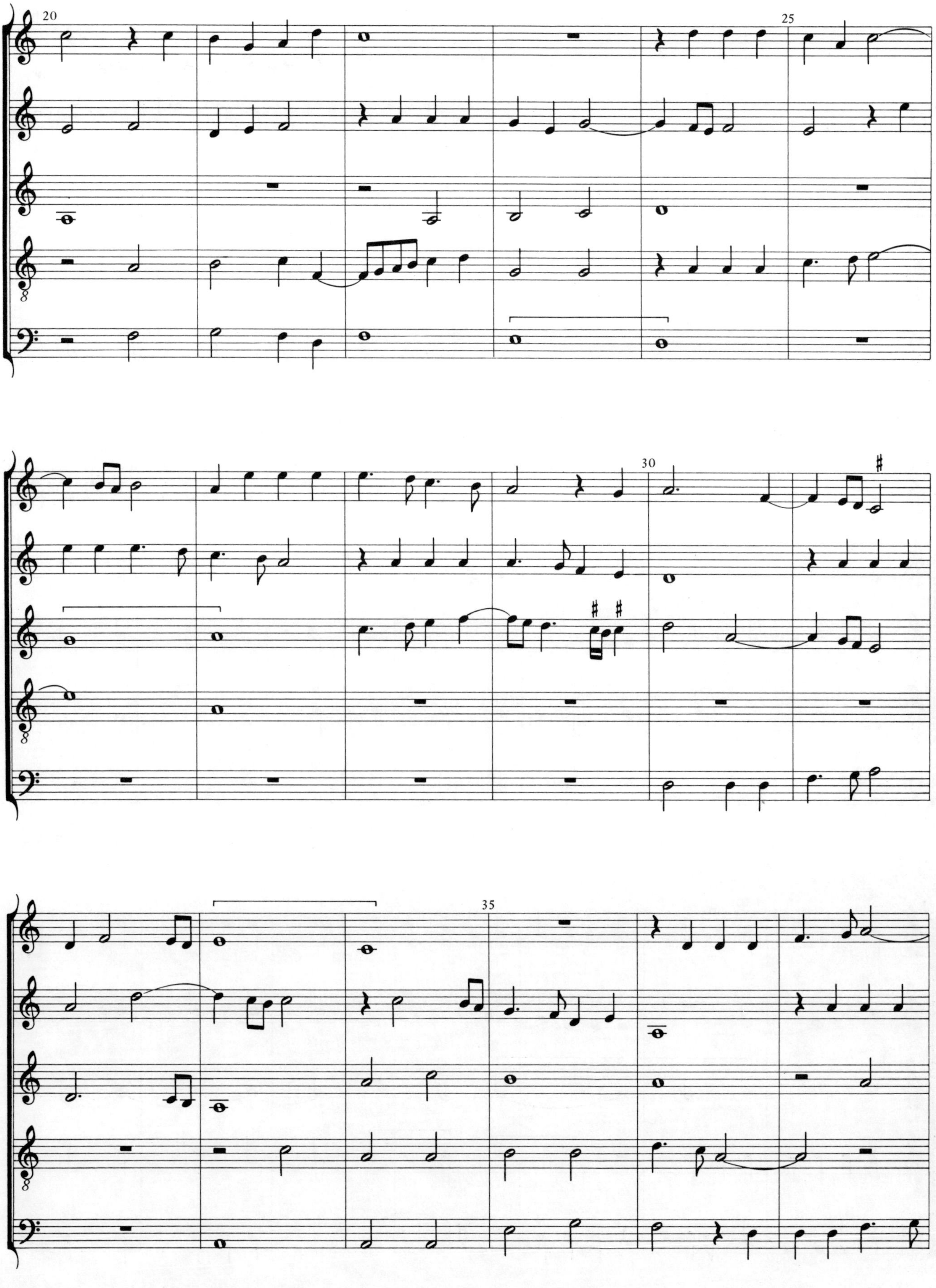
20
25
30
35

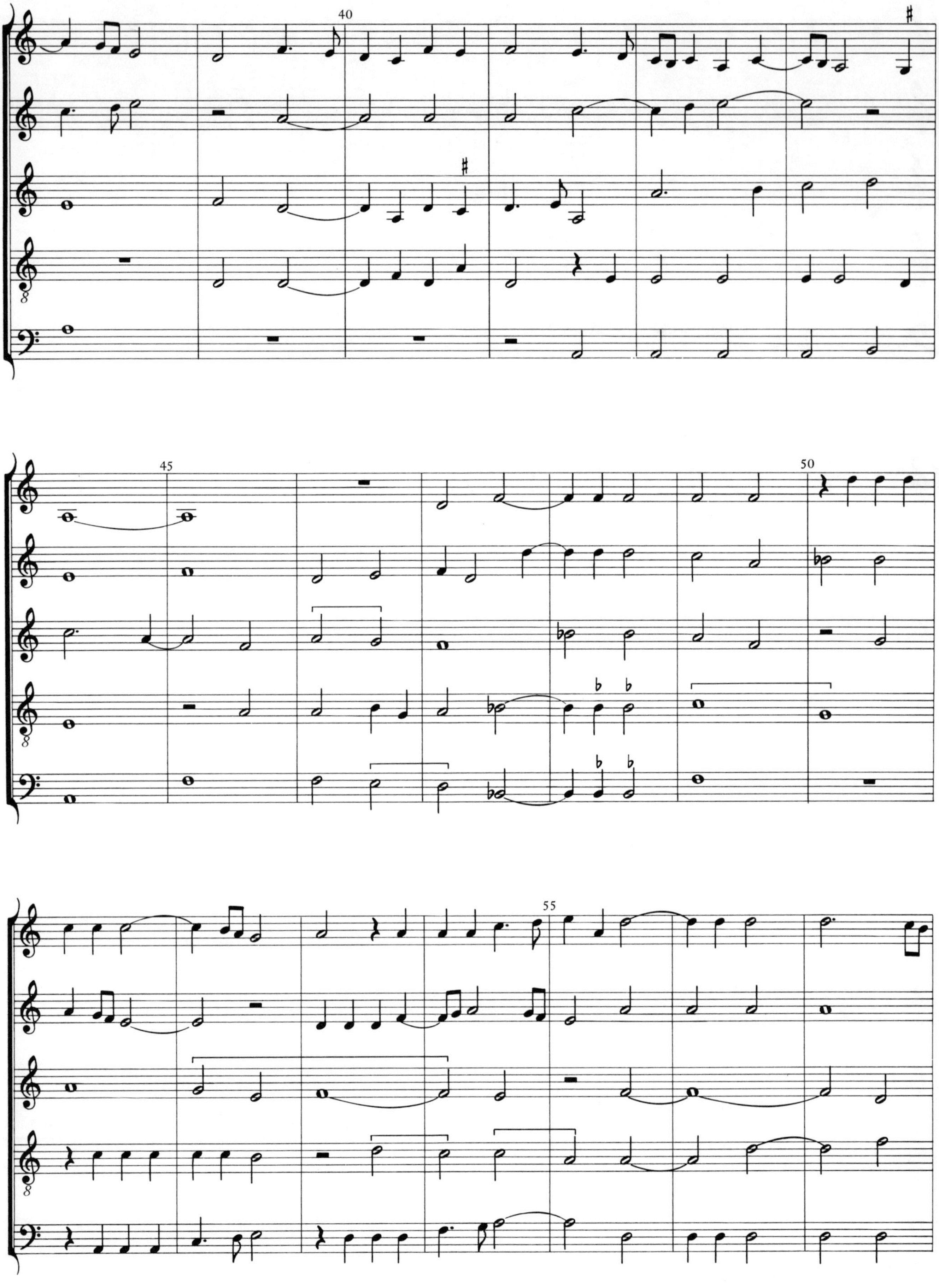
40
45
50
55

83

[24]

[Anonymous]

[Superius], [Tenor], [Contra]

Fors seulement l'attente que je meure, En mon las cueur [nul espoir ne demeure, Car mon malheur si tres fort me tour-

85

86

[25]

[Anonymous]

[Superius]

[Altus]

[Tenor] Fors seulement

[Bassus] Fors seulement

Vagans.*
Quinta Vox — Fors seulement

Fors seulement Primum

Fors seulement

---

* The *quinta vox* is not present in the principal source. It appears to be an added voice which the editor thinks is best omitted in performance.

87

88

[26]

[Matthaeus Pipelare]

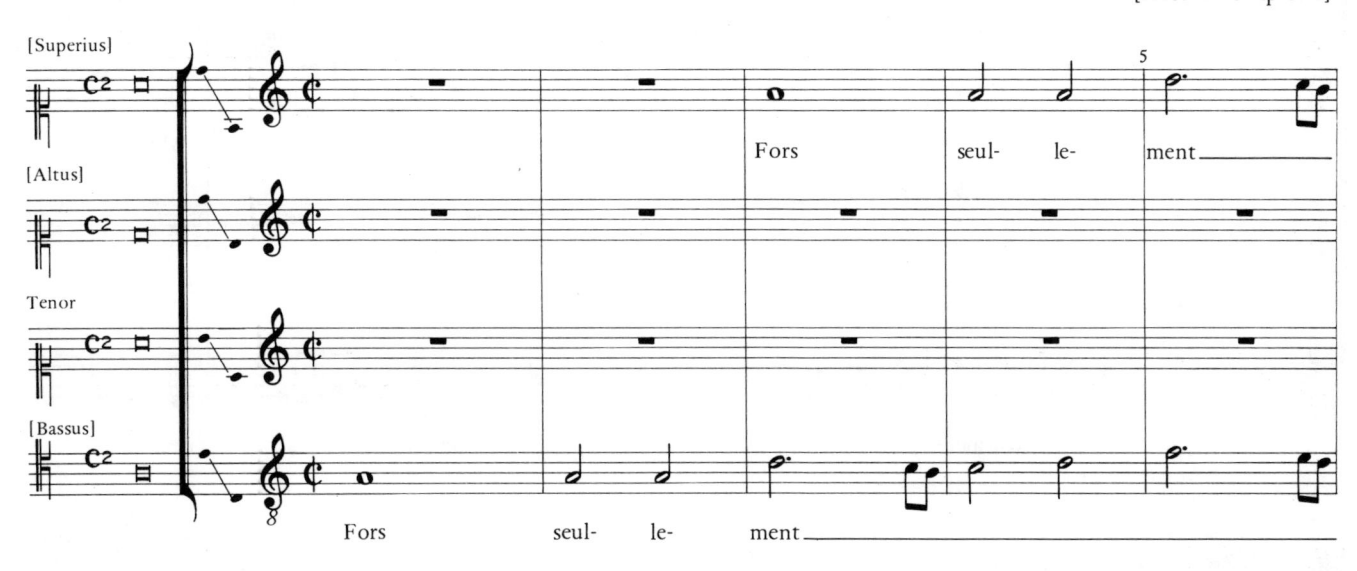

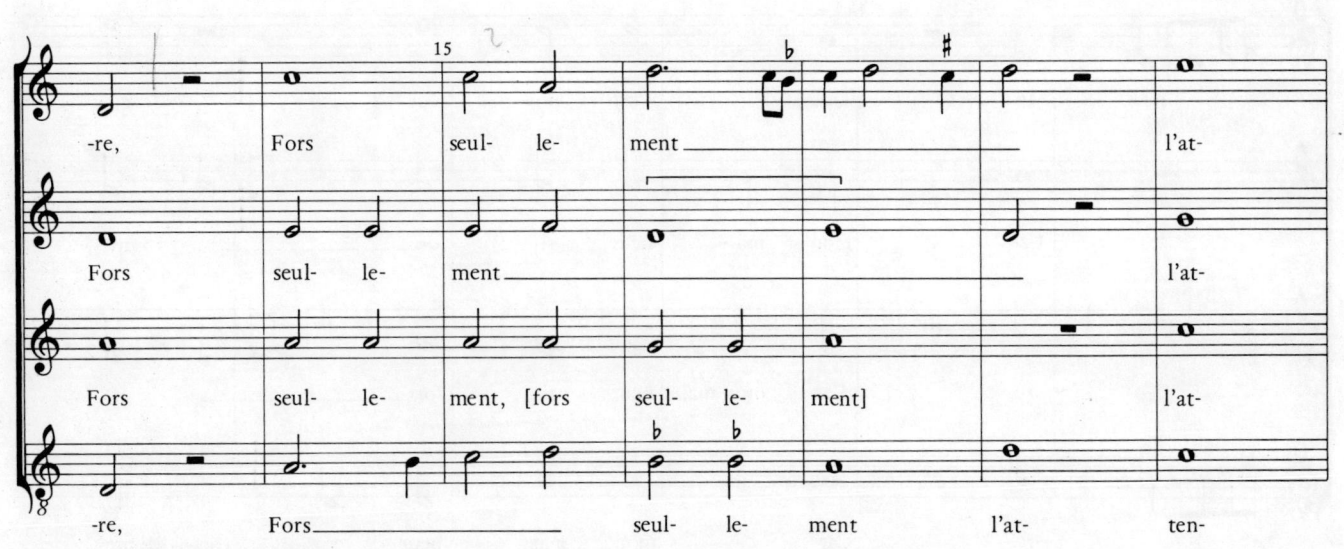

Lyrics by voice:

Voice 1: -ten- te que je meu- re, En mon las cueur nul e- -spoir ne de- -meu- re, Car mon mal- heur si fort me tour- -men- te Qui n'est do- leur que

Voice 2: -ten- te que je meu- -re, En mon las cueur nul e- spoir ne de- meu- re, Car mon mal- heur si fort me

Voice 3: -ten- te que je meu- -re, En mon las cueur nul e- spoir ne de- meu- -re, Car mon mal- heur si fort me

Voice 4: -te que je meu- -re, En mon las cueur nul e- spoir ne de- meu- -re, Car mon mal- heur si fort me

40
par vous je ne sen- te, que par vous je
tour-men- te Qui n'est do- leur
tour- men- te [Qui
tour-men- te Qui n'est do- - leur
45
50
ne sen- - te, Pour- ce que suis de
que par vous je ne sen- - te, Pour- ce que
n'est] do- leur que par vous je ne sen- te, Pour- -
que par vous je ne sen- te, Pour- ce que
55
vous per- dre bien seu- - re, bien seu- - re.
suis de vous per- dre bien seu- re.
-ce que suis de vous per- dre bien seu- - re.
suis de vous per- dre bien seu- - re.

[27]

[Anonymous]

[Superius]

[Altus]

Forseullement

[Tenor]

Forseullement

[Bassus]

Forseullement

Forseullement

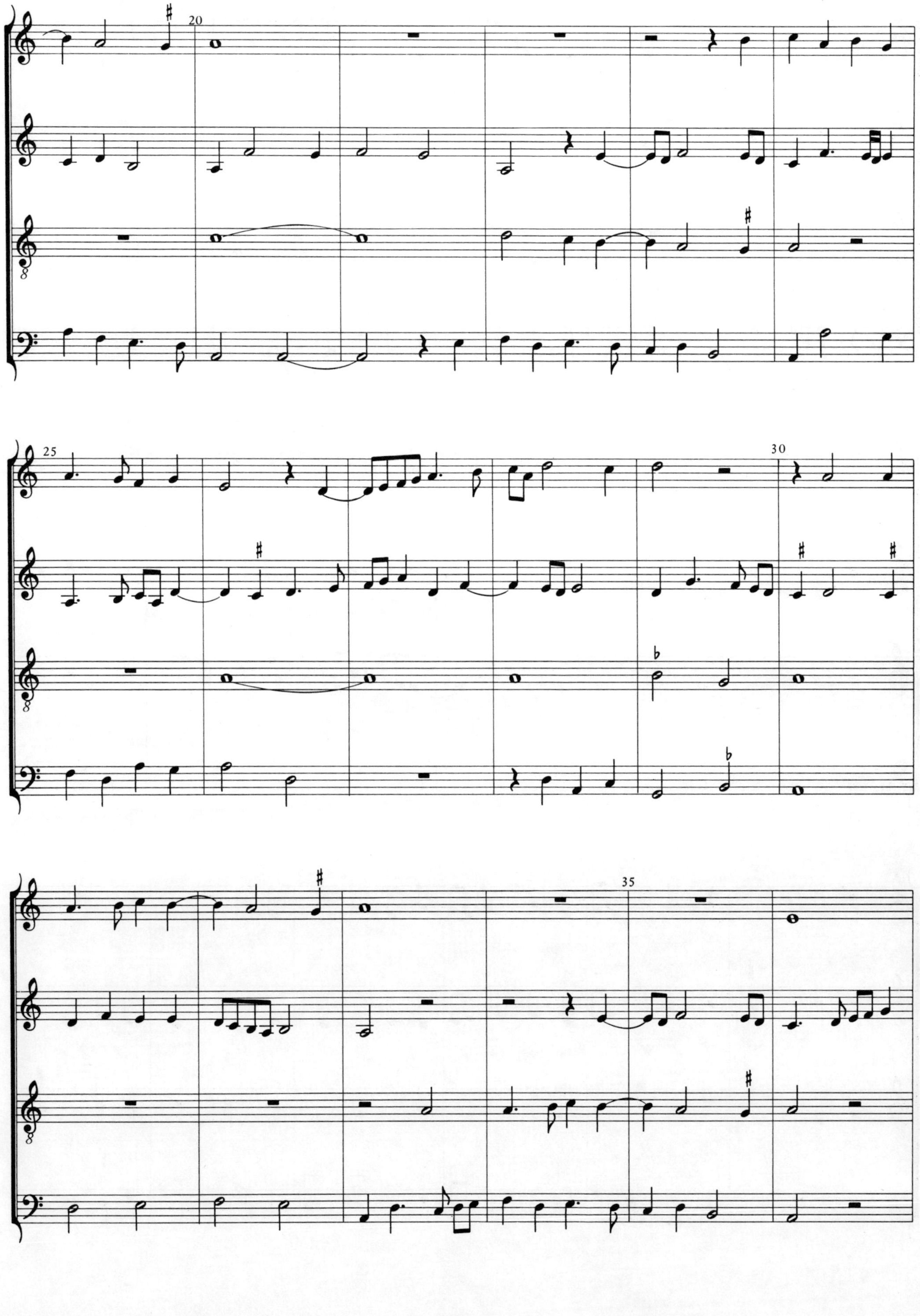
20
25
30
35

94

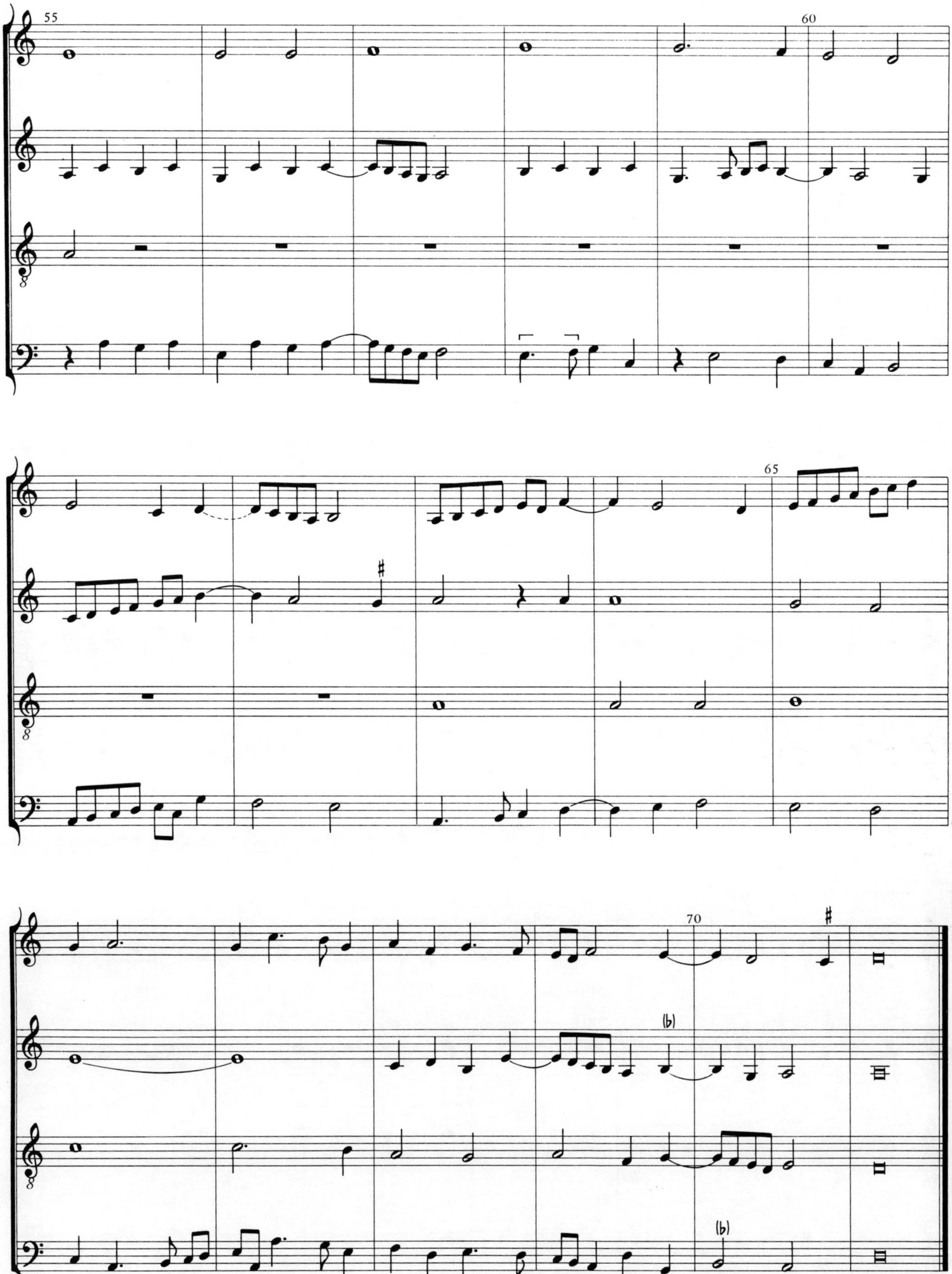

[28]

Anth[oine] de Févin

97

-chain d'en- nuy _____ et loing de son at-
-chain d'en- nuy _____ et
d'en- nuy et loing de son at- ten-

-ten- te, et loing de son at- ten-
loing de son at- ten- te, et loing de son at-
-te, et loing de son at- ten-

-te.
-ten- te.]
-te.

[29]

Jörg Blanckenmüller

[Superius] Forseulement

[Tenor] Forseulement

[Contra] Forseulement

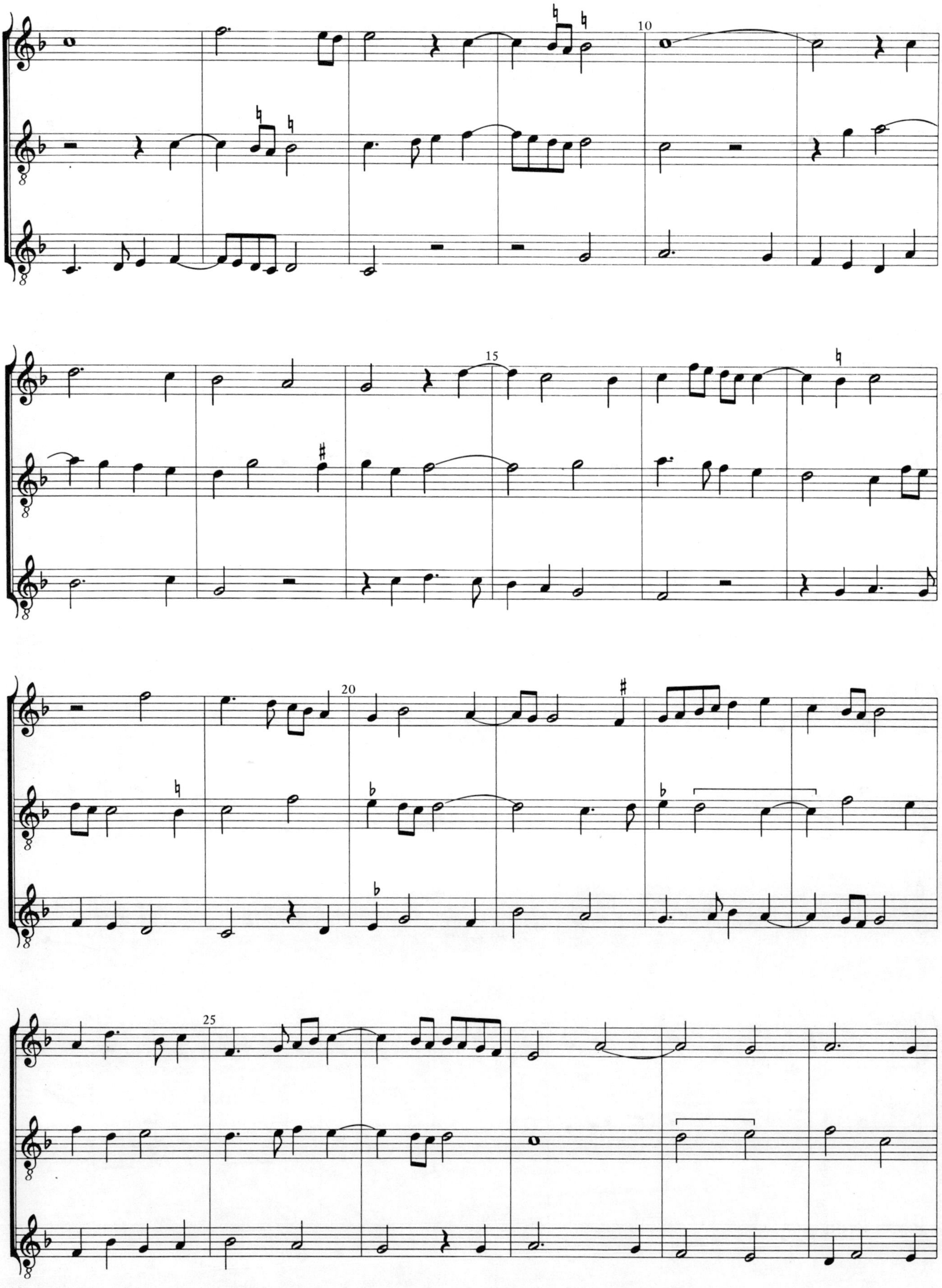
10
15
20
25

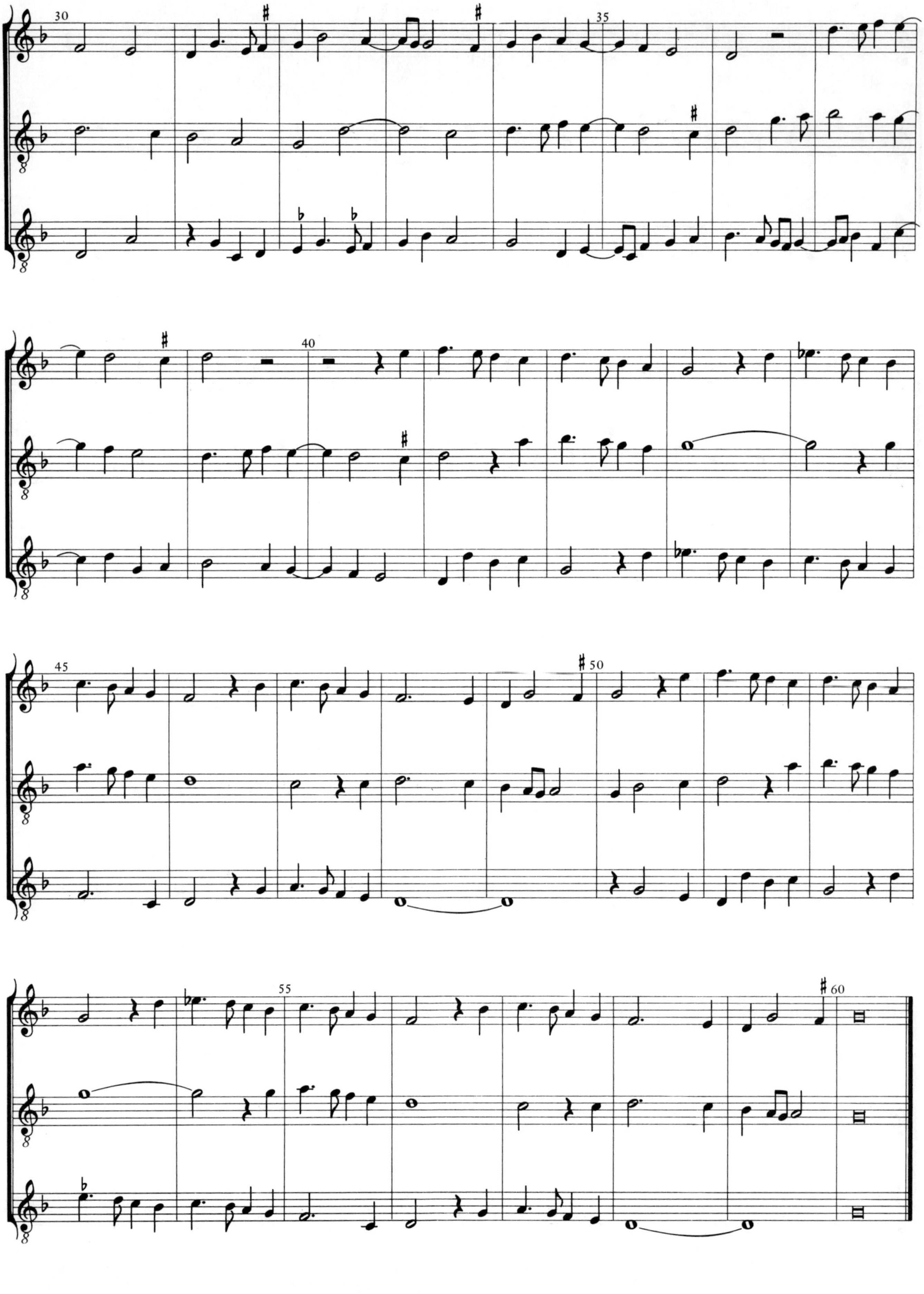

[30]

Adrianus Willa[e]rt

Ad equales voces

20
- se tan- te, Ay
soubz do- lo- reu- se tan- te, Ay
-tre at- ten- te De re- con- fort,
- lo- reu- se tan- te, Ay
do- lo- reu- se tan- te,
25
pris se jour de- pi- teu- se de-
pris se jour de- pi- teu- se de-
soubz do- - lo- reu- - se
pris se jour
Ay pris se jour de- pi- teu- se
30
- meu- re, de- pi- teu- - se
- meu- re, de- pi- teu- se,
tan- te, Ay
de- pi- - teu- se,
de- meu- re, de-

35
de- meu- re, de- pi- teu- se
de- pi- teu- se de-
pris se jour
de- pi- teu- se
-pi- teu- se de- meu- re, de- pi-
40
de- meu- re, Com- me ce- luy qui
meu- re,
de- pi- teu- se de- meu- re,
de- meu- re, de- meu- re, Com-
teu- se de- meu- re, Com- me ce- luy
45
so- le de- meu- re, de- meu- re
Com- me ce- luy qui so- le de- meu-
Com- me ce- luy qui so- le de- meu-
me ce- luy qui so- le de- meu- re,
qui so- le de- meu-

104

M2
.R2383
v.14